THE BIGGEST STORY

FAMILY DEVOTIONAL

❖❖ CROSSWAY

WHEATON, ILLINOIS

The Biggest Story® Family Devotional

Text © 2024 by Crossway

Illustration © 2021 by Crossway

Published by Crossway
        1300 Crescent Street
        Wheaton, Illinois 60187

All rights reserved. No part of this publication may be reproduced, stored in a retrieval system, or transmitted in any form by any means, electronic, mechanical, photocopy, recording, or otherwise, without the prior permission of the publisher, except as provided for by USA copyright law. Crossway® is a registered trademark in the United States of America.

Illustration and Cover Design: Don Clark for Invisible Creature, Inc.

First Printing 2024

Printed in China

Scripture quotations are from the ESV® Bible (The Holy Bible, English Standard Version®), © 2001 by Crossway, a publishing ministry of Good News Publishers. ESV Text Edition: 2016. Used by permission. All rights reserved. The ESV text may not be quoted in any publication made available to the public by a Creative Commons license. The ESV may not be translated in whole or in part into any other language.

All emphases in Scripture quotations have been added by the contributors.

ISBN: 978-1-4335-7981-3

Library of Congress Control Number: 2024939205

Crossway is a publishing ministry of Good News Publishers.

RRD		32	31	30	29	28	27	26	25	24
12	11	10	9	8	7	6	5	4	3	1

CONTENTS

Introduction ix
Ways to Use This Devotional x

PART 1: THE PENTATEUCH
GENESIS–DEUTERONOMY

1. And So It Begins *(Genesis 1–2)* 1
2. A Very Bad Day *(Genesis 3)* 5
3. From Bad to Worse *(Genesis 3–4)* 9
4. Rain, Rain, Go Away *(Genesis 6–9)* 13
5. A Table and a Tower *(Genesis 10–11)* 17
6. The Father of Nations *(Genesis 11–13)* 21
7. Let's Make a Deal *(Genesis 15; 17)* 25
8. The Judge Judges Justly *(Genesis 18–19)* 29
9. It's a Boy! *(Genesis 21–22)* 33
10. God's Tricky, Hairy, Blessed People *(Genesis 25; 27)* 37
11. Blessings in the Night *(Genesis 28; 32)* 41
12. Joseph's Mean Brothers and What God Meant to Do *(Genesis 37; 50)* ... 45
13. God Raises Up a Deliverer *(Exodus 1–3)* 49
14. Free at Last *(Exodus 4–15)* 53
15. The Way to Stay Free *(Exodus 19–20)* 57
16. A Fancy Tent and a Foolish Cow *(Exodus 32–34)* 61
17. A Tale of Two Goats *(Leviticus 16)* 65
18. Big People, Little Faith *(Numbers 13–14)* 69
19. You're Not the Boss of Me *(Numbers 16)* 73
20. The Daughters of Zelophehad *(Numbers 27; 36)* 77

PART 2: HISTORY
JOSHUA–ESTHER

21. The Walls Came Tumbling Down *(Joshua 6)* 81
22. The Fight of Gideon and the Flight of Midian *(Judges 6–7)* 85
23. Samson's Strength *(Judges 13–16)* 89
24. The Girl Who Wouldn't Go Away *(Ruth 1–4)* 93
25. The Lord's Word and Samuel *(1 Samuel 1; 3)* 97
26. The Rise and Fall of King Saul *(1 Samuel 8–15)* 101
27. David Stands Tall *(1 Samuel 16–17)* 105
28. David Sins . . . and Repents *(2 Samuel 11–12)* 109
29. The Wise and Foolish King *(1 Kings 3; 11)* 113
30. The Kingdom Cracks *(1 Kings 12)* 117
31. Elijah Proves a Point *(1 Kings 18)* 121
32. Grime and Punishment *(2 Kings 5)* 125
33. The Boy Who Sought the Lord *(2 Chronicles 34)* 129
34. Promises Broken and Promises Kept *(2 Chronicles 36)* 133
35. Walls and Worship *(Nehemiah 6–8)* 137
36. More Than a Pretty Face *(Esther 1–4)* 141

PART 3: POETRY
JOB–SONG OF SOLOMON

37. A Hard Life and a Good God *(Job 1)* 145
38. Cover Your Mouth *(Job 38–42)* 149
39. The Lord Is My Shepherd *(Psalm 23)* 153
40. The Beginning of Wisdom *(Proverbs 1)* 157

PART 4: THE PROPHETS
ISAIAH–MALACHI

41. What Isaiah Saw *(Isaiah 6)* 161
42. Jeremiah against Everyone *(Jeremiah 1)* 165

43. The Valley of Dry Bones *(Ezekiel 37)* 169
44. The Fiery Furnace *(Daniel 3)* 173
45. Writing on the Wall *(Daniel 5)* 177
46. The Miraculous Catnap *(Daniel 6)* 181
47. A Marriage Made in Heaven *(Hosea 1–3)* 185
48. Let Justice Roll Down *(Amos 5)* 189
49. Famine and Feast *(Amos 8–9)* 193
50. Big Fish, Bigger Mercy *(Jonah 1–4)* 197
51. A Change of Clothes *(Zechariah 3)* 201
52. The Great and Awesome Day of the Lord *(Malachi 3–4)* 205

PART 5: THE GOSPELS
MATTHEW–JOHN

53. A New Baby and a New Beginning *(Matthew 1)* 209
54. Wise Men, Smart Move *(Matthew 2)* 213
55. The Pointer and the Point *(Matthew 3)* 217
56. The Sin That Wasn't *(Matthew 4)* 221
57. The Sermon That Was *(Matthew 5–7)* 225
58. Mr. Clean *(Mark 1)* 229
59. Get Up! *(Mark 2)* 233
60. Follow the Leader *(Mark 3)* 237
61. A Story about Soils *(Mark 4)* 241
62. The Scary Boat Ride *(Mark 4)* 245
63. Send Us to the Pigs! *(Mark 5)* 249
64. A Sick Woman and a Sad Dad *(Mark 5)* 253
65. The Voice Is Silenced *(Mark 6)* 257
66. The Happy Meal That Kept on Going *(Mark 6)* 261
67. A Walk on the Water *(Matthew 14)* 265
68. A Dogged Faith *(Mark 7)* 269
69. Confessing Christ *(Matthew 16)* 273
70. Glory Mountain *(Matthew 17)* 277
71. The Kids Can Come Too *(Mark 10)* 281

72. Who Is My Neighbor? *(Luke 10)* 285
73. Lost and Found *(Luke 15)* 289
74. Debts and Debtors *(Matthew 18)* 293
75. Grumbles and Grace *(Matthew 20)* 297
76. Little Man, Big Faith *(Luke 19)* 301
77. The King Comes *(Luke 19)* 305
78. Jesus Cleans House *(Mark 11)* 309
79. A Woman to Be Remembered *(John 12)* 313
80. A Meal for the Ages *(Matthew 26)* 317
81. Everyone Leaves Jesus *(Mark 14)* 321
82. The Snake Crusher Is Crushed for Us *(Mark 15)* 325
83. Jesus Lives *(Luke 24)* 329
84. A Mission for the Ages *(Matthew 28)* 333

PART 6: ACTS AND EPISTLES
ACTS–JUDE

85. The Spirit Comes *(Acts 2)* 337
86. The Beautiful and the Beggar *(Acts 3)* 341
87. One Name under Heaven *(Acts 4)* 345
88. The Couple Who Lied and Died *(Acts 5)* 349
89. Stephen's Speech *(Acts 7)* 353
90. Philip and the Man from Africa *(Acts 8)* 357
91. Saul Sees the Light *(Acts 9)* 361
92. Peter Eats and a Soldier Believes *(Acts 10)* 365
93. Knock Knock, Who's There? *(Acts 12)* 369
94. Paul, Purple Goods, and a Prison Quake *(Acts 16)* 373
95. The God Who Can Be Known *(Acts 17)* 377
96. Ships and Snakes and Sermons, Oh My! *(Acts 27–28)* 381
97. No Nothing *(Romans 8)* 385
98. Love Is *(1 Corinthians 13)* 389
99. More Than a Slave *(Philemon)* 393
100. Taming the Tongue *(James 3)* 397

PART 7: REVELATION
REVELATION

101. Jesus Writes a Letter *(Revelation 1–3)* 401
102. The Center of the Universe *(Revelation 4–5)* 405
103. The Snake Crusher Wins *(Revelation 20)* 409
104. All Things New *(Revelation 21–22)* 413

Introduction

God calls all Christians—young and old—to learn, love, and live out his holy word. *The Biggest Story Family Devotional* is designed to help achieve that goal. Based on the stories found in Kevin DeYoung's *The Biggest Story Bible Storybook*, and featuring Don Clark's amazing artwork, *The Biggest Story Family Devotional* is divided into 104 stories—52 from the Old Testament and 52 from the New Testament. Each story features The Big Picture (an overview of the story), Gospel Connection (a summary of how the story connects to the good news about Jesus), a short prayer, and five readings and questions.

The five readings and questions can be done in one setting—perhaps Sunday night! Or, as that might be quite the challenge, you can break them out for a whole week. Do whatever best suits your family. The readings are short enough to have the readers in your family participate and the listeners, Lord willing, listen! And the questions are designed to generate an interesting conversation.

To achieve that goal, some of the questions ask about the content of the text (observations), others about the big ideas and message (interpretation), and some about practical ways to live out what you learn (application). Some questions are difficult (feel free to ask your older children to weigh in; or, please weigh in yourself) but most are simple—designed with the K–5th grade age group in mind. The "yes or no" questions are great for the youngest children. Let them answer yes or no and then, when it fits, follow up with "Why?"

Flexibility is the key word to keep in mind as you work through the devotional. Feel free to go fast or slow. Feel free to read more or less of the Bible readings. Feel free to skip questions or add your own.

May our great God bless your family as you read, discuss, and learn together God's wonderful word.

DOUGLAS SEAN O'DONNELL

Ways to Use This Devotional

This devotional provides a flexible way for families to meditate on God's word together. It is especially designed to help parents and children engage with the Bible text behind each of *The Biggest Story* Bible stories. Here are some options for how to use it with your family.

DINNER TABLE DEVOTIONS • 5–10 MINS • ALL AGES

At the beginning of the week, read The Big Picture and watch the animated story. Then for the next five days, read one of the five Bible readings and discuss the questions together. Close the week with the Gospel Connection and prayer. Each reading is designed to be short and doable for busy families with kids at various ages.

What you need: This devotional, a full English Bible, and a device for watching the animated story

LONGER EVENING DEVOTIONS • 30–40 MINS • OLDER KIDS

Families with older children may wish to do an entire devotion in one sitting, including all five Bible readings. If so, you might consider selecting a different reader for each reading and allowing them to take turns leading the discussion.

What you need: This devotional, a full English Bible, and a device for watching the animated story

ALONGSIDE *THE BIGGEST STORY BIBLE STORYBOOK*
10–15 MINS • YOUNGER KIDS

Families with younger kids may prefer to read from *The Biggest Story Bible Storybook* as the main focus of their Bible time together. You can use this devotional as a supplement to the storybook by simply selecting one or two discussion questions and reading the Gospel Connection after reading the story.

What you need: This devotional and *The Biggest Story Bible Storybook*

A note about the lines after each question: The lines provided after each discussion question can be used in different ways. Here are some suggested uses:

- Write down key points from your family's discussion to refer back to in subsequent readings.
- Mark the date and write down key questions or insights from individual family members. Used in this way, this book will become a family keepsake as you enjoy looking back on the contributions that each of your children bring to the discussion.

A screen-free alternative: In each of the use cases above, you may choose to read from *The Biggest Story Bible Storybook* instead of watching the animated video together. The content of the videos is the same as the stories printed in the storybook.

STORY 1

And So It Begins

GENESIS 1–2

THE BIG PICTURE: Genesis begins with God: "In the beginning, God" (Gen. 1:1). That's the first line of the Bible! Before "God created the heavens and the earth" (1:1), God was. He always was. But what did he do before he created everyone and everything? Was he lonely? No. Bored? Of course not. Scared? Certainly not. Why? God is one God in three persons—Father, Son, and Spirit. The three persons of the Trinity have always been marked by love, and it is out of this love that God created every person, place, and thing.

READING 1 • GENESIS 1:1–2

The Always Existing

Have you ever thought about the fact that God has no beginning? What questions do you have about that?

....

....

....

....

READING 2 • GENESIS 1:3–23

And God Said

Why do you think the Bible makes such a big deal of the fact that God created the world simply by speaking?

....

....

....

....

READING 3 • GENESIS 1:26–27

Made in God's Image

God made us in his image. We are supposed to reflect who he is. What are some ways we can mirror God to the world?

....

....

....

....

READING 4 • GENESIS 2:4–7, 18–25

Man and Woman

Why do you think God made Adam out of the ground? Why do you think God created Eve from Adam's rib?

....

....

....

....

READING 5 • JOHN 1:1–3

Creation and Salvation

John calls Jesus "the Word." Why is it important that all things were made *through* Jesus?

....

....

....

....

GOSPEL CONNECTION: The story of creation is just the first story of the Biggest Story. In Genesis we will learn that, because of sin, people aren't very good mirrors. We don't reflect God very well. But "the Word" (John 1:1) came as "the image of the invisible God" (Col. 1:15). He perfectly showed what God is like, and he made a way for our broken mirrors to be repaired so that we could again do the job God created us to do. But the Son of God isn't just our Savior. He, with the Father and the Spirit, created everything. Our Creator saves!

PRAYER: Dear God, we love to see all the good things in your creation. Thank you for making this world and for making us to be like you. Amen.

STORY 2

A Very Bad Day

GENESIS 3

THE BIG PICTURE: One day Satan, in the form of a snake, slithered into the garden. He wanted to get Adam to eat from the off-limits tree by tricking and deceiving Eve. His plan worked. Adam and Eve ate the forbidden fruit. The first sin. The worst sin in the world! Adam and Eve knew it. God too. It was a bad move and very bad day. God sent them out of the garden. And he cursed his perfect world. The ground would be hard. Work would be hard. Marriage would be hard. Having babies would be hard. And death would soon come to everyone.

READING 1 • GENESIS 3:1–5

Twisting God's Word

Would you be tempted by what Satan said? Why or why not?

READING 2 • GENESIS 3:6

The First Sin

The Bible teaches that Adam, not Eve, committed the first sin (see Rom. 5:12–21). Why do you think Adam is held responsible?

....

....

....

....

READING 3 • GENESIS 3:7–13

The Blame Game

Who did Adam blame for his sin? Do you ever blame others for your sin? Why do we do this?

....

....

....

....

READING 4 • GENESIS 3:14–24

Crime and Punishment

How did God punish the serpent, the woman, and the man? As a boy or girl, is there anything that scares you about those punishments?

....

....

....

READING 5 • ROMANS 5:12–14, 19

The Promise of the Snake Crusher

How are Adam and Jesus alike? How are they different?

....

....

....

....

GOSPEL CONNECTION: Genesis 3 records a very bad day. God cursed the snake, the man, and the woman. He promised that hardship and death would come to every human. (And it has!) But he also promised a fresh start. Adam and Eve would die, but not right away. Eve would have children. More than that (much more than that!), one of her offspring would deal with the snake (Gen. 3:15). Let's call him the Snake Crusher. We know him as Jesus. Satan would "bruise" Jesus (Jesus died). And yet, when Jesus died, he actually destroyed Satan. He crushed the snake! Yes, Jesus's worst day was our best day.

PRAYER: Dear God, we are sorry for all the lies we believe and all the bad stuff in our hearts. Thank you for the Snake Crusher, who gives us a new beginning. Amen.

STORY 3

From Bad to Worse

GENESIS 3–4

THE BIG PICTURE: Genesis 3 teaches us how sin and death came into the world. It also gives the wonderful promise that God would send the Snake Crusher to crush, well, the snake! But before we talk about that good news, we need to look at Genesis 4, which tells us about some very bad news and sad news. Life outside of Eden goes from bad to worse. Adam and Eve have two boys—Cain and Abel. That sounds great! But the problem is that neither one of them is the Snake Crusher. The bigger problem is that Cain crushed his own little brother. He murdered him. How terrible!

READING 1 • GENESIS 4:1–2

Cain and Abel

Who was born first? What different jobs did they have?

....

....

....

....

READING 2 • GENESIS 4:3–7
Cain's Offering

Hebrews 11:4 teaches us that Cain's offering was sinful because it wasn't offered with faith in God's promises. Why is it wrong to make an offering to God without faith?

....

....

....

....

READING 3 • GENESIS 4:8–16
Am I My Brother's Keeper?

When God asked Cain where his brother was, how did Cain respond? Was that the right response?

....

....

....

....

READING 4 • GENESIS 4:17–24
East of Eden

Cain's pathway leads to Lamech. Did he sound like a good person? Why or why not?

....

....

....

....

READING 5 • 1 JOHN 3:12

The Way of Cain

According to the apostle John, why did Cain kill Abel?

....

....

....

....

GOSPEL CONNECTION: Adam and Eve must have missed Eden. Now they lived without God's daily presence and with sin and death everywhere. But what hope did they have? Could they just fight the mighty angel and return to the garden? No. Could they fly to heaven to be with God? Of course not! All that they could do was trust God's promise. God would not leave his people in this curse forever. Yes, God so loved us that he sent Jesus, the Snake Crusher. And Jesus so loved us that he paid for our sins by dying on the cross. Now, if we believe in him, we can walk with God and talk with God. A return to Eden! Better than Eden.

PRAYER: O Lord, please help us to turn away from evil. We want to learn to trust you. Save us from our sin and from ourselves. Amen.

STORY 4

Rain, Rain, Go Away

GENESIS 6–9

THE BIG PICTURE: *Good. Good. Good. Good. Good. Good. Very Good.* Remember those words? God said them at creation. But ever since Adam and Eve ate from the off-limits tree, the words *bad, bad, bad, bad, bad, bad, very bad* best describe what happened next. It was bad that Eve got tricked by the serpent. Bad that Adam disobeyed God. Bad that Cain killed his brother. And by Noah's day, people were so very bad that God sent a great flood to wipe out everyone evil from the face of the earth. Only Noah and his family were spared, because they trusted in God's word and hoped in his promise.

READING 1 • GENESIS 6:5–10
What God Saw

When God looked down upon the earth, what did he see? What did he decide to do?

....

....

....

....

Story 4 • Rain, Rain, Go Away • 13

READING 2 • GENESIS 6:11–19

The Ark

What did God ask Noah and his family to do? Do you think that would have been hard or easy to do? Why?

....

....

....

....

READING 3 • GENESIS 7:11–24

Two by Two

Who shut the door to the ark, and why is that important? How many days and nights did it rain, and what do you think that would have been like? Who was in the ark with Noah? Would you have liked being in the ark?

....

....

....

....

READING 4 • GENESIS 9:8–17

God's Covenant

Do you like rainbows? What can your family do to remember God's covenant whenever you see a rainbow?

....

....

....

READING 5 • HEBREWS 11:3–7

By Faith

Did you recognize any of the people or events from our readings in Genesis? How did those people show faith?

....

....

....

....

GOSPEL CONNECTION: Our day is not so different than Noah's day. Some people ignore God. Other people hate God. And lots of people hate one another. Well, God does not like this, and he has promised to judge all sin. One day, he will destroy all that is not good—not with water (remember the rainbow?) but with fire. But there is the good news—what the Bible calls the gospel. If we come to Jesus, we will be saved from the coming judgment, just like Noah was saved. And we too will have a new beginning.

PRAYER: God, we know you have a right to be angry with us when we sin. We are glad you haven't given up on us but have sent Jesus to save us. Amen.

STORY 5

A Table and a Tower

GENESIS 10–11

THE BIG PICTURE: Why are there so many nations? And why are there so many languages? Over six thousand today! And why do so many Chinese people speak Mandarin, so many Russians speak Russian, and so many Saudi Arabians speak Arabic? The Bible shares a story about how God created the nations, gave people different languages, and scattered them around the world. It might sound like a fun story. But it's actually another sad story. Or, it starts fun and ends sad. It starts with God's image bearers keeping God's command to be fruitful and multiply. But it ends with God's image bearers' wanting to make themselves as great as God, instead of showing how great God is.

  Watch Story 5 together

READING 1 • GENESIS 10:1, 32

The Sons of Noah

After you read the first and last verse of Genesis 10, look at all the names found in between those verses. Maybe count the names and try to say a few of them. What were the names of Noah's three sons?

....

....

....

READING 2 • GENESIS 11:1–4

Let Us Make a Name for Ourselves

What are two reasons the people wanted to build the tower?

....

....

....

....

READING 3 • GENESIS 11:5–9

Its Name Was Called Babel

What did God think of this plan? What did he do about this plan? Why?

....

....

....

....

READING 4 • GENESIS 11:10, 29–30

Over the Face of the Earth

After you read the beginning and end of this genealogy, look at all the names found between those verses. What was Abram and Sarai's sad struggle? Do you know anyone who has that same struggle?

....

....

....

....

READING 5 • ACTS 2:1–8; REVELATION 7:9–12

Behold, a Great Multitude

In Acts 2:1–8 what did God do differently from what he did in Genesis 11:1–9? In Revelation 7:9–12 how many people praised God in a loud voice? Were they from just a few nations, speaking just a few languages? What did they all shout?

....

....

....

....

GOSPEL CONNECTION: When Jesus came, he didn't just save his own nation (the Jews), but people from every language and tribe and nation (the Gentiles). This is what happened: First, people from Jerusalem believed in him. Then, people from the Middle East, Africa, and Europe. Then, people from the Americas and Asia. From the North Pole to the South! And it's still happening today. Someday, in heaven, God will be praised by people from every nation in languages that all God's people will understand. And, then and there, we will finally work together to show just how amazing God is.

PRAYER: O God, sometimes we like to think we are bigger than you. We're sorry. Thank you for caring about people from every nation on the earth. Amen.

STORY 6

The Father of Nations

GENESIS 11–13

THE BIG PICTURE: Do you remember God's rescue plan? It was the Snake Crusher, who would come from Eve. Soon enough, Seth was born. Later Noah. Then Noah's son Shem. And from Shem's family came Abram (later called Abraham). Abraham was from a place called Ur. That town's funny name sounds like *fur*, just as God's *plan* sounds like Abra*ham*. Abra*ham* would be God's *man* to carry out God's *plan*. The plan was awesome. God would give Abraham a Promised Land. He would also give him lots of children. And through one of those children God's promise to save and bless people from every nation would come true.

READING 1 • GENESIS 12:1–3

God's Amazing Promises

What did God ask Abraham to do? What did God promise him? (See if you can list all the blessings.)

....

....

....

....

READING 2 • GENESIS 12:4–9

Abraham's Response

Did Abraham obey God? Do you think that was hard or easy? Why?

....

....

....

....

READING 3 • GENESIS 12:10–20

In Egypt

Abraham started out so well. But does it sound like he's trusting God in this story? Why or why not?

....

....

....

....

READING 4 • GENESIS 13:1–18

Giving Lot a Lot

What did God promise Abraham after he let Lot have the better land? What does this teach us about God?

....

....

....

....

READING 5 • GALATIANS 3:15–16, 27–29

The Promised Offspring

Who is the offspring? How did we become part of Abraham's offspring?

....

....

....

....

GOSPEL CONNECTION: God made Abraham some amazing promises! And at that time, Abraham had no idea how God would keep these promises. But the rest of the Bible tells us how. God gave Abraham a son, Isaac. Then Isaac had a son who had lots of sons. Soon, Abraham's children and grandchildren and great-grandchildren were a great nation called the people of Israel. God led Israel to the Promised Land and gave it to them, just as he said he would. But there is more to the story. God kept adding people to the family. When Jesus came, he made a way so that all the families of the earth could be part of God's family—even people who weren't Israelites. They became known as Christians. And Jesus promised he was going to prepare a place for them—a new and better promised land.

PRAYER: We thank you, God, for all your promises and all the blessings that are ours in Jesus. Amen.

STORY 7

Let's Make a Deal

GENESIS 15; 17

THE BIG PICTURE: God called Abraham to leave his home for the Promised Land when he was seventy-five years old. And God promised him that, if he did so, then he would have both the land and a son. In Genesis 15–17 Abraham was in the land, but his family lived in only a small part of it. And he had his wife, but still no son. Abraham was now much older, and he began to wonder, "Will God really keep his promise to do the impossible?" God knew Abraham's doubts. So, one dark night, he brought Abraham outside and said, "Look up, and count the stars. I will give you as many children and grandchildren and great-grandchildren as there are stars in the sky" (see Gen. 15:5). Let's read about what else happened.

READING 1 • GENESIS 15:1–6

Big Promises, Great Faith

What were the big promises God made to Abraham? How did God respond to Abraham's doubts? How did Abraham respond to God?

....

....

....

READING 2 • GENESIS 15:7–18

Cutting a Covenant

Why did God have Abraham cut a bunch of animals in half?

....

....

....

....

READING 3 • GENESIS 16:1–6

Like a Yo-Yo

Abraham's life was sometimes like a yo-yo. One day, he was close to God, believing his promises, and the next day he was far from God, doubting his promises. In this passage, where are Abraham and Sarah in their relationship with God—believing God's promise for a son or doubting it? Do you ever feel like a yo-yo with God? How so?

....

....

....

....

READING 4 • GENESIS 17:1–10

The Sign of Circumcision

After such an amazingly gracious promise, God asked Abraham to show that he believed. He asked him to show it through a special sign called circumcision. This special sign would remind all his family after him that they were chosen and loved. Do Christians have a special sign that shows us that we belong to God? Why do you think that sign is so important?

READING 5 • GALATIANS 3:13–14

Sons of Abraham

Gentiles are non-Jewish people. How does the blessing of Abraham, the father of the Jews, come to people who aren't Jews (Gentiles)?

GOSPEL CONNECTION: "[Abraham] believed the LORD, and he counted it to him as righteousness." What? Sinners like Abraham could be counted righteous? People under the curse that Adam and the snake unleashed could be made right with God? (This is what *right*eous means.) How could this be? The answer is through faith. When Abraham believed God's promise, he was counted as righteous. He wasn't counted righteous because he was such a good person. He wasn't counted righteous because he was so religious. He was counted righteous because he believed God. To put it differently, he was saved by faith.

PRAYER: O God, help us to believe your word, and help us to be patient when we aren't sure what's going to happen or what to do. Amen.

STORY 8

The Judge Judges Justly

GENESIS 18–19

THE BIG PICTURE: Each time Abraham doubted and disobeyed, God came to him and reminded him of their covenant. One day the Lord said to Abraham, "This time next year, Sarah shall have a son." When Sarah heard what God said, she laughed because she couldn't believe that she would have a child when she was so old. She doubted God and even lied to God: "I did not laugh." In these chapters we will learn that Sarah wasn't the only sinner. There was a whole city full of sinners. And we will see that, while God promises good things for his people (he forgives sinners), he also promises to punish his enemies (he judges sinners).

READING 1 • GENESIS 18:1–15

Laughing at the Lord

Who appeared to Abraham? What was promised? What would happen in a year's time?

....

....

....

....

READING 2 • GENESIS 18:16–33

Anyone Righteous?

What does it show about God's heart that he agreed to Abraham's requests?

....

....

....

....

READING 3 • GENESIS 19:12–22

God Saves

What did the two angels tell Lot and his family to do? Why might it have been hard for Lot's family to obey the angels? Why was it important for them to obey, even though it was hard?

....

....

....

....

READING 4 • GENESIS 19:23–29

God Judges

What did God do to Sodom and Gomorrah? What happened to Lot's wife and why?

....

....

....

....

READING 5 • 2 PETER 2:6–10a

God Knows How to Rescue

According to this passage, what will happen to the ungodly? How about the godly?

....

....

....

....

GOSPEL CONNECTION: God knows, hates, and judges our sins. But God also offers to forgive all our sins in Jesus, the Snake Crusher who crushed all our sins on the cross. We may not come from a city filled with people who do bad things all the time. But that does not mean we are perfect. In fact, there are many sins we all do every day. Just as we saw with Sodom and Gomorrah, God will judge all the earth justly. But God also gives us a way to escape—just like he did with Lot's family. That way is Jesus!

PRAYER: Dear God, please show us our sins. Lead us to hate our sins. And forgive ours in Christ. Amen.

STORY 9

It's a Boy!

GENESIS 21–22

THE BIG PICTURE: Let's review some of the stories in Genesis. God created everything—persons, places, and things. Solar systems and stars too! God put Adam and Eve in a beautiful garden on earth. They loved God and they loved each other. How lovely! When Adam disobeyed, God banished Adam and Eve from the garden of Eden. How unlovely. But God still loved his people and had a plan to rescue them. Part of that *plan* involved God's calling of Abra*ham*. God promised Abraham that he would be a blessing to all the families of the world. That blessing would come through the birth of a son.

READING 1 • GENESIS 21:1–7

Birth of the Promised Son

What are some different reasons people laugh? Why did Sarah laugh?

....

....

....

....

READING 2 • GENESIS 21:8–21

Hagar and Ishmael

What did Sarah and Abraham do to Hagar and Ishmael? How did God respond to sad Hagar? What does this teach us about God?

....

....

....

....

READING 3 • GENESIS 22:1–8

The Offering

God promised Abraham that Isaac was the one through whom blessing would come. What does it show about Abraham's view of God (and his promises!) that he obeyed God's strange command?

....

....

....

....

READING 4 • GENESIS 22:9–19

The Provision

When God told Abraham to sacrifice his son, it seemed as though God wouldn't keep his promise. How did God ultimately keep his promise?

....

....

....

READING 5 • ROMANS 8:31–39

Graciously Gave

How can we know that God loves us?

....

....

....

....

GOSPEL CONNECTION: The story of Abraham's (almost) sacrifice of his son, Isaac, is an amazing story. An even more amazing story is the story of God the Father's (actual) sacrifice of his son, Jesus. Isaac's story took place on a small mountain; Jesus's story took place on a hill. Abraham's beloved son would carry wood for the sacrifice; God's beloved Son would carry a wooden cross. Isaac's life was spared because God provided a ram (a male lamb) to be sacrificed in his place. But for Jesus, there would be no ram. Jesus was the sacrifice. He was the Lamb of God, who took away the sins of the world and rescued us from death.

PRAYER: We thank you, Father, for sending the promised child to be born of Mary and die for our sins. Amen.

STORY 10

God's Tricky, Hairy, Blessed People

GENESIS 25; 27

THE BIG PICTURE: By the time we get to where we are in Genesis, Adam and Eve's family tree has become quite large. From Seth came Noah. From Noah's son Shem came Abraham. Abraham married Sarah, and they had a son, Isaac, who married a girl named Rebekah. And, like Sarah, Rebekah had a hard time having a baby. Isaac prayed and the Lord heard his prayer: Rebekah became pregnant with twin boys. Imagine how big her belly was! They named their first son Esau; they named the second Jacob. We learn about them and their stories today.

READING 1 • GENESIS 25:7–11

Father Abraham

Can you think of someone really important who died? How was Abraham's death different?

....

....

....

READING 2 • GENESIS 25:19–26

Twins!

Why did your parents name you what you're named? How did Esau and Jacob get their names?

....

....

....

....

READING 3 • GENESIS 25:27–34

Trick Me Once

Why do you think Esau foolishly traded his birthright for some soup? Can you think of a time when you made a similar mistake?

....

....

....

....

READING 4 • GENESIS 27:1–29

Trick Me Again

God promised to bless Jacob. But his sneaky brother (and his sneaky mom) thought they had to steal the blessing. Do you ever feel like you have to look out for yourself instead of trusting God? Why is that?

....

....

....

READING 5 • MATTHEW 1:1–2, 17–21

Name above All Names

Why did God name his son "Jesus" when he came to earth? What does that tell us about Jesus?

....

....

....

....

GOSPEL CONNECTION: Do you know how the New Testament begins? Sure you do! We just read it. It begins with Jesus's family tree: "Abraham was the father of Isaac, and Isaac the father of Jacob" (Matt. 1:2). From that trunk comes over forty more names. And the final names listed? "Joseph the husband of Mary, of whom Jesus was born" (1:16). Our Savior who came to "save his people from their sins" (1:21) came *from* (and *for!*) sinners like Rebekah and Jacob. Listen and learn: the Biggest Story isn't about God's people getting it right as much as it's about God blessing his people even when they get things wrong.

PRAYER: We are glad, O God, that you don't help those who help themselves. You help us despite ourselves. Thank you. Amen.

STORY 11

Blessings in the Night

GENESIS 28; 32

THE BIG PICTURE: Do you remember the last devotion, in which we talked about the trickster twin and the two stories about how sneaky he was? Twice Jacob stole his father Isaac's blessings from Esau. Have you ever had someone take something really special from you? I bet you felt sad, hurt, or mad. The Bible tells us that after Esau learned Jacob stole his blessing he was mad. So mad that he wanted to kill Jacob. Rebekah told Jacob to leave town: "Get out of here now and stay with my brother Laban until Esau cools down." Today we read about what happens next to the brothers.

READING 1 • GENESIS 28:10–22

Jacob's Ladder

God promises to go with Jacob wherever he goes. Why is that such a special promise?

....

....

....

....

Story 11 • Blessings in the Night • 41

READING 2 • GENESIS 29:16–20

Jacob Marries Rachel (and Leah!)

Jacob was surprised to find he'd married Leah instead of Rachel. The trickster had been tricked! Have you ever had a disappointing surprise? What was it?

....

....

....

....

READING 3 • GENESIS 32:22–32

The Wrestling Match

Jacob leaves his fight with God with a permanent limp. Was this a good thing or bad thing? Why do you think so?

....

....

....

....

READING 4 • GENESIS 32:3–8; 33:1–4

So We Meet Again

If you were Jacob, how would you have felt about seeing Esau again? How did Jacob feel?

....

....

....

READING 5 • MATTHEW 1:18–25

God with Us

Can you think of any connections between this passage and the ones we've read about Jacob? Is there a connection between the ladder and Jesus as "Immanuel"? Is there a connection between sneaky Jacob and our need for a Savior?

....

....

....

....

GOSPEL CONNECTION: Did trickster Jacob deserve God's blessings? Of course not. Do we deserve the blessings that we have in Jesus—forgiveness of sins, a new heart, the Holy Spirit within, a big family (the church)? Of course not. What good news that in Jesus God makes his home with us! We learned that Jesus's name means "Savior" because he saves. He is also called Immanuel, which means "God with us." Jesus did not use a ladder to travel from heaven to earth, but he did travel from heaven to earth. Why? To be Savior and Immanuel. Isn't it wonderful that God saves and is always with us?

PRAYER: Lord, do not leave us alone. We need your help. We need a blessing. Help us to see that when we are weak, then you are strong. Amen.

STORY 12

Joseph's Mean Brothers and What God Meant to Do

GENESIS 37; 50

THE BIG PICTURE: Jacob had twelve sons. Joseph was the firstborn son of beautiful-eyed Rachel—so his father, Jacob, favored him. Jacob's favorite son quickly became the least favorite brother. His eleven brothers hated him. And after Joseph told them his dreams about their bowing down before him, they really hated him. What the brothers did next was terrible. And although really bad things happened in Joseph's life—he was thrown in a pit, sold into slavery, falsely accused, and sent to prison—God was with him. God had a plan for him, and through that plan he would actually save even his cruel brothers.

READING 1 • GENESIS 37:1–11

Joseph's Big Dreams

What did Joseph's brothers and father think of his dreams? What do you think about their reactions? Do you think Joseph's dreams will come true?

....

....

....

READING 2 • GENESIS 37:17–28

Joseph's Big Bad Brothers

What did Joseph's brothers do to him? What do you think Joseph thought about in the pit? What would you think about? Where did he end up?

READING 3 • GENESIS 39:20–23; 41:25–41
Bonus Reading: 42:1–6; 45:1–11

Joseph's Rise to Power

Read and briefly retell what happens to Joseph in Genesis 39–44, then ask: why did Joseph rise to power? Who was with him and gave him the wisdom he needed to survive and thrive? Who is with us and gives us wisdom?

READING 4 • GENESIS 50:15–21

God Meant It for Good

What did Joseph's brothers ask from him? How did Joseph respond?

READING 5 • ACTS 2:22–41

Jesus's Death—Our Good!

Like Joseph, Jesus was treated very badly by others. In fact, he was killed. How did God use Jesus's death for good? How did the people in Acts respond to Peter's sermon? How should we?

GOSPEL CONNECTION: In Genesis 50:20, Joseph gives the perfect summary of his story: "You meant evil against me, but God meant it for good, to bring it about that many people should be kept alive, as they are today." That verse can also be used to summarize the story of Jesus. Evil happened to him. He was rejected. Beaten. Mocked. Killed. And as he hung on the cross, it sure looked like evil won. But Jesus rose from the dead. He conquered sin. He crushed the snake. He took what the world meant for evil and brought about the greatest good. Our salvation!

PRAYER: Thank you, God, for working all things according to your perfect plan. Help us to trust you and to cling to the cross of Christ. Amen.

STORY 13

God Raises Up a Deliverer

EXODUS 1–3

THE BIG PICTURE: The story of Joseph has a happy ending. Genesis, however, ends on a sad note: "Joseph died" (Gen. 50:26). The book of Exodus starts on the same sad note: "Joseph died" (Ex. 1:6). And while Israel's next generation had lots and lots of children ("the people of Israel were fruitful and increased greatly; they multiplied and grew exceedingly strong, so that the land was filled with them," 1:7), matters went from bad to worse, and sad to sadder. "There arose a new king [Pharaoh] over Egypt, who did not know Joseph" (1:8). This new king made God's people slaves. They were slaves for over four hundred years! So very sad.

READING 1 • EXODUS 1:6–14

Enslaved in Egypt

What happened after Joseph died? Why did this happen? How would you feel if you were the Israelites?

....

....

....

....

READING 2 • EXODUS 1:15–2:10

Into the Nile

What did Pharaoh command to be done to the Israelite baby boys? Did all the women delivering babies obey that command? What does that tell us about whom they feared more—God or Pharaoh? How should we be like these brave women? What happened to baby Moses?

....

....

....

....

READING 3 • EXODUS 2:11–15

Moses—the Murderer!

What did Moses do? Why was he then afraid? What did he do next? What would you have done if you did what Moses did?

....

....

....

READING 4 • EXODUS 2:23–3:14

The Burning Bush

The Israelites were treated very badly. Had God forgotten about them? What did God do to show that he had not forgotten about them? Whom did he say he would use to deliver the Israelites? Whom did God send to deliver us?

....

....

READING 5 • JOHN 6:35; 8:12, 58; 10:9, 11; 11:25; 14:6; 15:1
Read them all, or pick a few

Who God Is

God calls himself "I AM WHO I AM" (Ex. 3:14). This means he always was and always will be. What a very big God! How is that different than any other person in the world? Eight times in John's Gospel, what words does Jesus use of himself? What does that teach you about him?

GOSPEL CONNECTION: When our Lord Jesus, the eternal Son of God, came to earth, he sometimes called himself "I AM"—the same words God used when he was talking to Moses! Jesus told the Pharisees, "Before Abraham was, *I am*" (John 8:58). Jesus existed before Abraham because he has always existed, and he will exist forever. And he exists forever to deliver his people. Just as God called Moses to deliver Israel from their slavery in Egypt, God sent Jesus to deliver sinners from their sins. "Thanks be to God," the apostle Paul writes, "that you who were once slaves of sin have . . . been set free from sin" (Rom. 6:17–18). In Jesus, we are rescued from sin so we can live for him—the great "I AM."

PRAYER: Thank you, Lord—the great "I AM"—for hearing our cries, caring about our troubles, and saving us. Amen.

STORY 14

Free at Last

EXODUS 4–15

THE BIG PICTURE: God saw Israel's suffering, and he came up with a plan to save them. Remember the burning bush? Remember when our always-and-forever God called himself "I AM WHO I AM" (Ex. 3:14)? This God said to Moses: "I am the God of Abraham, Isaac, and Jacob. I have seen the affliction of my people who are in Egypt, and I have come to deliver them out of the hand of the Egyptians and to bring them up out of Egypt into a land flowing with milk and honey" (see 3:6–8). God always keeps his promises. Exodus 4–15 records the exciting story of the promised rescue.

Watch Story 14 together

READING 1 • EXODUS 7:1–15
A Hard Heart

What was Pharaoh's response to God's command to let his people go? What happened when he refused to obey? What does this teach us about how we should respond to God's commands?

....

....

....

READING 2 • EXODUS 11:1–10

The Ten Plagues

Can you name the ten plagues? Which one would be the worst for you?

....

....

....

....

READING 3 • EXODUS 12:21–29

The Passover

What happened when the Israelites put the blood of a lamb over their doorposts? What happened to those who had no lamb's blood on their homes?

....

....

....

....

READING 4 • EXODUS 14:21–15:3

The Lord Drove the Sea Back

How did God save Israel? What happened to Pharaoh and his army? How did Israel respond to such a great salvation? Is there a song that you like to sing to God?

....

....

....

READING 5 • MATTHEW 26:17, 26–29; 1 CORINTHIANS 5:6–8

Jesus, Our Passover Lamb

What are we saved from when we trust that the blood of Jesus perfectly covers our sin? How is Jesus like the lamb in the exodus story?

....

....

....

....

GOSPEL CONNECTION: Have you noticed a pattern in how God works? Trouble before triumph. Suffering before salvation. Danger before deliverance. The story of our rescue in Jesus is no different. He is rejected by his people. He is arrested, sentenced to die, mocked, spit on, slapped, and finally crucified on a cross. Trouble. Suffering. Danger. But the story isn't over. Next comes triumph, salvation, and deliverance! Jesus rises from the dead. He triumphs over the grave. Jesus saves everyone who believes in him. And he will return to deliver us from trouble, suffering, and danger.

PRAYER: O great God, we praise you for delivering us and setting us free. Amen.

STORY 15

The Way to Stay Free

EXODUS 19–20

THE BIG PICTURE: Remember when God passed over houses with the lamb's blood on their doorposts? Remember when he opened and closed the Red Sea when the Israelites were leaving? God commanded his people to remember this rescue. Once a year the Israelites had a feast called Passover to celebrate what God had done in saving them from slavery and death. But the command to remember wasn't the only good command God gave. In Exodus 20 God gave Israel the Ten Commandments. These ten rules show God's people what it means to love God and love people. They are good rules that free us to serve our good and gracious God.

READING 1 • EXODUS 19:7–14

Getting Ready to Meet God

What were the people to do to prepare to meet God? What does this teach you about God's character? Do we have to do the same thing to enter into God's presence? If not, why not?

....

....

....

READING 2 • EXODUS 19:16–20

God Shows Up!

When God came on the mountain to meet with Israel, did he come to them in a quiet whisper? How do you think you would react if you were there that day at the foot of the mountain?

....

....

....

....

READING 3 • EXODUS 20:2

Saved to Serve

What did God do first—save his people from their slavery in Egypt or give them the Ten Commandments? Why is the order important?

....

....

....

....

READING 4 • EXODUS 20:2–17

The Ten Commandments

How many of the Ten Commandments do you know by heart? What command do you not understand? What command do you struggle to keep?

....

....

READING 5 • MATTHEW 22:34–40
Two Great Commandments

How does Jesus summarize the Old Testament commandments of God? What does that teach you about what matters most to God?

GOSPEL CONNECTION: God didn't give the Ten Commandments and then save Israel. First he saved Israel, then he gave the Ten Commandments. The same pattern is true today. God doesn't tell us to be good so that he can save us. Instead, he saves us first, as a gift. Because of God's great love, Jesus came into the world to save us from the power of the devil and forgive all our sins. But Jesus saves us for a reason: to be a special people (a kingdom of priests and a holy nation) who love God and love others.

PRAYER: Dear God, thank you for your word. Help us to walk in your ways. For your glory and for our good. Amen.

STORY 16

A Fancy Tent and a Foolish Cow

EXODUS 32–34

THE BIG PICTURE: God delivered his people out of slavery in Egypt. Then he saved them from the Egyptians. The Israelites crossed the Red Sea. The Egyptians, however, did not. Their chariots are buried in the mud under millions of gallons of water. Next, he gave his people the Ten Commandments, ten rules to keep them free. Ten rules that taught them to love God and love others. But, what do you think? Do you think God's people will keep his great rules? No, just like Adam and Eve, they won't. Today we will hear a story about a cow that almost killed a nation.

READING 1 • EXODUS 32:1–6

The Golden Calf

Why did the Israelites make a golden calf? Are you ever tempted to worship something other than God? If so, what or who?

....

....

....

READING 2 • EXODUS 32:7–14

God's Response to Their Worship

God was upset and wanted to consume his people in his holy anger. How did Moses stop God from destroying the people?

....

....

....

....

READING 3 • EXODUS 33:7–11, 18–23

The Tent of Meeting

Who met Moses in the tent? What did Moses want to see? If you had a direct meeting with God, what would you talk to him about?

....

....

....

....

READING 4 • EXODUS 34:29–35

Down from the Mountain

What did Moses look like when he came down from the mountain? Why did he look that way? What does this teach us about God?

....

....

....

READING 5 • 2 CORINTHIANS 3:7–18

The Veil Is Removed

How many times is the word *glory* used in this section of Paul's letter? How is the veil removed? Put differently, how do we now behold God's glory?

....

....

....

....

GOSPEL CONNECTION: Earlier in Exodus, Israel had been saved from the big, bad Egyptians. But now Israel came face-to-face with another enemy: the sin within them. Salvation comes when God defeats his enemies, but salvation also comes when God is gracious and merciful with us in our sin. But why was God able to forgive Israel? Was it simply because Moses was such a good mediator? No. There had to be something more. And that more would come in Jesus, when he paid the penalty for our sin. Do you know we have the same enemy as the Israelites? No, not the Egyptians. Our own sin. So we need the same rescuer—Jesus!

PRAYER: Forgive us, O God, for worshiping puny gods like everyone else. Show us your glory and make us shine for you. Amen.

STORY 17

A Tale of Two Goats

LEVITICUS 16

THE BIG PICTURE: God gave his people laws about sacrifices. Some of the sacrifices were offered as thanksgivings to God; other sacrifices were offered to pay for sins against God. One day a year the holiest person in Israel (the high priest) would put on his holy clothes (called garments) and go into the holy tent to stand before our holy God and make a sacrifice for God's unholy people. This special day—called the Day of Atonement—was a *holy* day, kind of like the *holi*days of Christmas, Easter, and, especially, Good Friday. The priest's job that day was to offer a special sacrifice for sin.

READING 1 • LEVITICUS 16:1–4
Coming into the Holy Place

What was Aaron told to do? What would happen if he didn't do as commanded? If you were Aaron, would you be afraid to make this sacrifice?

....

....

....

....

Story 17 • A Tale of Two Goats • 65

READING 2 • LEVITICUS 16:5–19

Sacrifices for Sins

What animal did Aaron sacrifice for his and his family's sins? What animal did he sacrifice for God's people? Do you think there was a lot of blood in the tent of meeting on the Day of Atonement? What do you think God is teaching his people through these sacrifices?

....

....

....

....

READING 3 • LEVITICUS 16:20–22

The Scapegoat

What is the point of the goat that is set free in the wilderness?

....

....

....

....

READING 4 • LEVITICUS 16:29–34

A Statue Forever

How many times does the word *atonement* appear in this section of Scripture? What does that word mean? Why is it so important then and now?

....

....

....

READING 5 • HEBREWS 4:14–5:5; 7:26–27

Bonus Reading: 9:13–14; 10:4–10

A Great High Priest

What are the differences between Aaron and Jesus as high priest? Between their sacrifices? To whom should we go to deal with our sins?

....

....

....

....

GOSPEL CONNECTION: Like a street sign that tells you, "This way to New York," the two goats we read about that were sacrificed and spared point to Jesus. Like the first goat, Jesus would die for our sins. He was our sin substitute: "For our sake [God] made [Jesus] to be sin who knew no sin, so that in him we might become the righteousness of God" (2 Cor. 5:21). Like the second goat, Jesus's death would cause our sins to be forgotten. Because of Jesus—the only perfectly holy man, our high priest—God says, "I will be merciful toward their iniquities, and I will remember their sins no more" (Heb. 8:12).

PRAYER: We thank you, God, for sending Jesus to die for our sins so that we can have a relationship with you. Amen.

STORY 18

Big People, Little Faith

NUMBERS 13–14

THE BIG PICTURE: Moses sent twelve spies into the Promised Land. They returned with some good news: Milk. Honey. Figs. Pomegranates. The world's *biggest* grapes! They also gave some bad news. Ten of the spies said, "The *big* cities have *big* walls guarded by *big* people. We will look like grasshoppers! We can't go into the land. They'll crush us under their *big* feet!" The people cried out loudly in fear. Joshua and Caleb, two of the spies, disagreed. They said, "The people are *big*. True enough. But our God is so much *bigger*. Listen, our big God is with us, and he will give us the land!" Whom will Israel listen to?

READING 1 • NUMBERS 13:1–3, 17–20

Spy Out the Land

Read verse 2 again. What did God promise to give Israel? What did Moses send the twelve spies out to do? List as many tasks as you can remember. Would you be excited or afraid, or a mix of both, to go on their spy mission?

....

....

....

READING 2 • NUMBERS 13:25–33

Two Reports

What was the report from the ten spies? What was Joshua and Caleb's report? Why do you think some of the spies were afraid and Joshua and Caleb weren't? Should you be afraid when God calls you to do difficult things?

....

....

....

....

READING 3 • NUMBERS 14:1–10

The People Grumbled

Joshua and Caleb told God's people not to fear because God delights in them and promised to give them the land. Did the people listen to the two spies or the ten? What did they want to do? What did they want to do to Joshua and Caleb? Do you ever find it hard to believe God's promises and follow his leaders?

....

....

....

....

READING 4 • NUMBERS 14:10–24

God's Mercy and Judgment

How happy do you think God was with Israel's decision *not* to enter the land? *Not* so happy. In fact, God was angry. Moses had to step in again. He prayed for the people. And once again, God did not destroy the people like they deserved. But he still punished those who doubted God after all he had done for them. What was their punishment? Do you think that was a fair punishment?

....

....

....

....

READING 5 • REVELATION 21:1–4; 21:22–22:5

A Better Promised Land

Where did God promise to bring the Israelites? Where has God promised to bring those who believe in Jesus, the Lamb? How is the new heaven and new earth described? What do you most look forward to in living there forever?

....

....

....

....

GOSPEL CONNECTION: We are a lot like Israel. Too often we doubt God's promises and are too afraid to do the hard things he calls us to do. But Caleb and Joshua teach us what true faith looks like. True faith is brave. It trusts that God will keep his promises. So what do we do when our faith is small? There is a simple prayer we learn from Mark 9:24. It goes like this: "I believe. Help my unbelief." Even such small faith in a big, promise-keeping God is enough because God is, well, big!

PRAYER: We are sorry, Lord. Too often we doubt your promises and are too afraid to do the hard things you call us to do. Help us believe! Amen.

STORY 19

You're Not the Boss of Me

NUMBERS 16

THE BIG PICTURE: Moses set the people free from slavery. He gave them the Ten Commandments. He performed signs and wonders. And twice, when God was about to destroy them, Moses prayed to God and asked him to forgive the Israelites instead of destroying them. Moses had been an amazing leader and had done all that God asked him. And the people loved him for it, right? Wrong. They didn't see what was so special about Moses. Wasn't he a person just like them? Again and again they rebelled against him as their leader and insisted, "You're not the boss!"

READING 1 • NUMBERS 16:1–4

The Rebels

Who rebelled against Moses and Aaron? Why?

....

....

....

....

....

READING 2 • NUMBERS 16:5–11

Why Grumble against Us?

Moses told the rebels to come to the tabernacle for a showdown. God would show up to this showdown and decide who would serve as his holy priest—Aaron and his sons ("the sons of Levi") or these rebels. How do you think Moses felt when he invited these rebels to the showdown? How would you have felt?

....

....

....

....

READING 3 • NUMBERS 16:18–35

The Showdown

Whom did God side with? How did God judge the rebels? If you were one of the people watching this, what would you do?

....

....

....

....

READING 4 • NUMBERS 16:41–48

More Grumbling, More Grace

Who saved God's people from God's judgment? How?

....

....

READING 5 • HEBREWS 10:11–14

Our High Priest

How are Jesus and Aaron alike? How is Jesus greater?

GOSPEL CONNECTION: Like Moses and Aaron, Jesus was rejected. People hated him so much that he was crucified. But on the cross, like Aaron, he asked for forgiveness for God's people ("Father, forgive them, for they know not what they do," Luke 23:34). Like Aaron, he did this by making atonement for their sins ("Christ . . . offered for all time a single sacrifice for sins," Heb. 10:12). Aaron risked his life to save the Israelites, but Jesus actually died and gave his life to save his people. Jesus is so much greater than Aaron; he is our great Savior and high priest!

PRAYER: Father in heaven, help us to trust you and to trust those you send to be our leaders. Most of all, give us faith to trust in Jesus. Amen.

STORY 20

The Daughters of Zelophehad

NUMBERS 27; 36

THE BIG PICTURE: The Bible is a big story—you could even say it's the Biggest Story! And within the Biggest Story are lots of little stories. There are famous stories like Noah and the flood and Moses crossing the Red Sea. But the Bible also has lots of less famous stories. Do you think the less famous stories are unimportant? No! "All Scripture is breathed out by God and profitable for teaching, for reproof, for correction, and for training in righteousness" (2 Tim. 3:16). Put differently, each and every page of the Bible is important and will help us to know, love, and follow God.

READING 1 • NUMBERS 27:1

Ze-loph-e-had

First things first. Say "Za," which rhymes with *baa* and *cha, cha, cha*. Say "loaf," like a loaf of bread. Say "uh," like you're about to ask a question. Say "had," like I just *had* to eat my veggies. Put those four sounds together and what do you get? Ze-loph-e-had! Had you heard of Zelophehad before today? What were the names of his five daughters?

....

....

....

READING 2 • NUMBERS 27:2–4

Give to Us

What happened to Zelophehad? What did his daughters want?

....

....

....

....

READING 3 • NUMBERS 27:5–11

A New Rule

Did Moses know what to do when the daughters first came to him? Whom did he turn to for help? Whom should we turn to first when we need help? Do any of you have a story where God helped you? What decision did Moses make? What does that decision teach us about God?

....

....

....

....

READING 4 • NUMBERS 36:2–3; 10–12

Marry the Right Man

Did the daughters of Zelophehad keep God's plan and marry the right man from their own clan? When you get married, should you marry a person who loves and follows Jesus?

....

....

READING 5 • 1 PETER 1:3–5

A Better Inheritance

By trusting Jesus, we will receive his wonderful inheritance. How is this inheritance better than what the daughters received?

GOSPEL CONNECTION: The story of Zelophehad's daughters is really a story about the Promised Land. When God told Isaac he would give him and his offspring the land, the promise was for Zelophehad and his daughters too. And do you know who else will inherit a promised land? Everyone who trusts Jesus. We don't inherit the same land that the five girls did. We inherit heaven, a place completely without sin. When you think about how Zelophehad's inheritance passed to his daughters, remember that Jesus's inheritance passes to us. Pretty important for a not-so-famous story!

PRAYER: We thank you Lord for every story in the Bible and all that we learn from your word. Amen.

STORY 21

The Walls Came Tumbling Down

JOSHUA 6

THE BIG PICTURE: After Moses died, God chose Joshua to lead his people into the Promised Land. The Lord said to Joshua, "Just as I was with Moses, so I will be with you. I will not leave you or forsake you. Be strong and courageous" (Josh. 1:5–6), for Joshua had to take over and destroy every city in the land. Joshua obeyed God. And the people followed his lead. They said, "All that you have commanded us we will do, and wherever you send us we will go" (1:16).

READING 1 • JOSHUA 5:13–15

The Commander of the Lord's Army

Why did the commander ask Joshua to take off his shoes? Do you think Joshua and Israel's army will need the help of the commander of God's army? Do we need God's help in our battles against our enemies, especially temptations to sin?

....

....

....

READING 2 • JOSHUA 6:1–5
Strong and Courageous

What promise did God make to Joshua? Was it an easy promise to believe? Would you have a hard time doing what God asked Joshua to do? What fears might you have?

....

....

....

....

READING 3 • JOSHUA 6:15–20
The Walls Fell Down

March around your kitchen table seven times, blow a horn (if you have one!), and then shout, "The Lord has given us the city!" Was that fun? Silly? Why do you think God had his people do what might have seemed like such a silly thing?

....

....

....

READING 4 • JOSHUA 6:17, 22–25
Saved Alive

Was Rahab saved from destruction because she was a good person or because she believed the word of God—that the Lord was giving her evil city to the Israelites? How are we saved from eternal destruction?

....

....

READING 5 • 1 CORINTHIANS 15:24–26

Victory in Jesus

What is the last enemy that Jesus will destroy? Could we defeat that enemy without him? How does the fact that you will live forever make you feel?

GOSPEL CONNECTION: God's people have always faced enemies. Sometimes they are people who oppose God and his ways. Other times they are things like sin, death, and Satan. Through Jesus all our enemies will be defeated. Sin forgiven. Death killed. Satan crushed. And, yes, people brought down in judgment. Hallelujah! We have the victory in Jesus! And someday soon we will enter a far better promised land than the city of Jericho. In the new heavens and new earth there will be never-ending peace, love, and joy. All-you-can-eat food too! But the best part will be our never-ending face-to-face fellowship with our commander: Jesus Christ.

PRAYER: O God, you do amazing things. Thank you for fighting our battles. In you we have victory over death. Amen.

STORY 22

The Fight of Gideon and the Flight of Midian

JUDGES 6–7

THE BIG PICTURE: Israel's history is like a teeter-totter: up and down, down and up. Israel rebels and God disciplines. They cry out for help and God rescues. They grow comfortable and start sinning again. And then the whole thing repeats itself. This pattern is especially true in the book of Judges, which records stories about the time of the judges—God's leaders who ruled after Moses and Joshua. These judges didn't wear black robes, bang gavels, and say, "Order in the court!" They were warrior-rulers. And when they relied on their own strength, they lost their battles. But when they relied on God's strength, they were victorious.

READING 1 • JUDGES 6:1–6
Cried Out for Help

Why did Israel cry out to God for help? Do you ever cry out to God for help? If so, what sort of help do you ask for?

....

....

....

READING 2 • JUDGES 7:14–16

An Answer to Prayer

Judge Gideon was the answer to the people's prayer. Did Gideon think he was strong enough to do what God asked him to do? What did he (and we!) need to know about God?

....

....

....

....

READING 3 • JUDGES 7:36–40

A Strange Sign

Gideon had a lot of fears. When God asked Gideon to battle the Midianites, how did Gideon gain the courage he needed to obey? Put differently, what were the signs that God was with him? Should we ask God for such signs today?

....

....

....

READING 4 • JUDGES 7:2–8

The Big Battle

Gideon and his army will win the big battle. Before that, what did God do to Gideon's big army before the battle? Why do you think God chose a weak judge and a small army to win his battle?

....

....

READING 5 • EPHESIANS 6:10–17

Strong in the Lord

Who is the enemy we are up against? Would you rather have the armor of God to protect you or twenty thousand strong soldiers? As a family, pretend to put on the armor of God. For example, say "helmet of salvation" and pretend to place a helmet on your heads.

GOSPEL CONNECTION: "In those days there was no king in Israel. Everyone did what was right in his own eyes." Four times in the book of Judges a similar refrain appears. One of the best promises that God gave us was the promise of a coming king. This king would save God's people. This king would lead God's people. This King is Jesus, the Snake Crusher. Without King Jesus, we'd all be our own kings, doing whatever it is we think is right. But King Jesus changes our hearts so that we actually want to do, and have the courage to do, what God wants.

PRAYER: We trust you, O Lord. Give us courage to do what you ask of us. Amen.

STORY 23

Samson's Strength

JUDGES 13–16

THE BIG PICTURE: Joshua had led God's people into the Promised Land—the land flowing with milk and honey. But there was still a big problem: there were lots of bad people living in the land. God brought judgment on these people by raising up judges. Remember how the Midianites were defeated by Gideon? He and the other judges led God's people in battles to defeat their enemies in the Promised Land. This helped them remember God's promises and receive them. The most famous of these judges was Samson. He was so famous because he was so strong! He was also famous because he was sinful.

READING 1 • JUDGES 13:21–25
What God Gives

Samson's parents, before they were parents, struggled to have a baby. Then one day, the Lord told Samson's mother, "You shall conceive and bear a son" (Judg. 13:3). Then she had Samson! Who gives life and strength? Why it is important that we understand this truth?

....

....

....

READING 2 • JUDGES 14:5–6

Super Strong

What amazing thing was Samson able to do with God's strength? If you just exercise enough, can you be as strong as Samson? Why was he so strong? Where should we find our strength?

....

....

....

....

READING 3 • JUDGES 16:19–21

Samson and Delilah

Why did Samson lose his strength? The Bible names two reasons. Do you think his long hair is where he got his super strength?

....

....

....

....

READING 4 • JUDGES 16:28–30

Strengthen Me

What evil things did the Philistines do to Samson? How did God judge them for all the evil things they did? Should we pray for what Samson prayed for?

....

....

READING 5 • HEBREWS 12:1–2

The Only Superhero

Who are some of your heroes who love Jesus? What are they like? Is any of them perfect? Who is the one perfect superhero who saves us from our sins?

GOSPEL CONNECTION: Jesus is the Bible's only superhero. He is not a superhero just because he can do things that most people cannot do, like walk on water. He is a superhero because he is *super good*. The best heroes in the Bible set an example for us, but they all have weaknesses. Only Jesus was without sin. Only he made the ultimate sacrifice. Like Samson's enemies thought they defeated Samson, God's enemies thought they had defeated God. But unlike Samson, Jesus wasn't captured because he was foolish. And unlike Samson, Jesus didn't stay dead! He rose again. He conquered his enemies and ours—sin, death, and the devil. He is the only superhero we need.

PRAYER: Help us, God, to learn from our heroes. Lead us to the only hero who can save us from our sins. Amen.

STORY 24

The Girl Who Wouldn't Go Away

RUTH 1–4

THE BIG PICTURE: In the days of the judges, bad things happened. Bad things like a famine. Bad things like an Israelite family leaving the Promised Land for a foreign country. Bad things like a husband and two children dying. Things were so bad that one woman, Naomi, even changed her name to Bitter. But God is working even in the bitter times. God used Bitter's family to bring his blessing to a foreign woman—like how he brought a blessing to Rahab. And this was exactly like how he'd promised Abraham that he was going to bless all the people of the earth through him.

READING 1 • RUTH 1:1–5, 15–17

Your God Shall Be My God

How did Ruth, a Moabite, demonstrate faith in the Lord, the God of Israel (the true, living, and only God)? Do you turn to the Lord when times are hard?

....

....

....

READING 2 • RUTH 2:1–12

A Harvest of Love

How did Ruth and Boaz meet? What did Boaz like about Ruth? Do you want to get married someday? What should you look for in a husband or wife?

READING 3 • RUTH 3:8–13

Redeemed

The word *redeem* means to save. Boaz would redeem Ruth (and Naomi!) from their bitter life by marrying Ruth. Who is the greater Redeemer? What does he save us from?

READING 4 • RUTH 4:13–17

First Comes Marriage, Then Love

Then (sometimes) babies! What is the name of Ruth's baby? Take a guess: Why do you think this baby is important? Do you want to have children someday? What would you call them, and why would you pick those names?

....
....
....

READING 5 • MATTHEW 1:1–6, 17

Jesus's Family Tree

What are the names of your parents and grandparents? Why is it important that Jesus has a family tree? Do you recognize any of the names in his family tree? Jesus is called the "son" of whom?

....
....
....
....

GOSPEL CONNECTION: Ruth and Boaz's son (Obed) had a son (Jesse) who had a son (David). David was the king Israel was waiting for—a king after God's own heart. Not the perfect king. Only Jesus is the perfect King. But a king that helped God's people do what is right in God's eyes. From King David comes King Jesus, our Redeemer who saves us from our sins and brings us new life. As you just read, Matthew starts with a list of names, Jesus's family tree. And do you know whose name is in that list? Ruth! God's plans are so much better than we can ever imagine.

PRAYER: You always have a plan, God, even when things don't seem right. We trust you. Amen.

STORY 25

The Lord's Word and Samuel

1 SAMUEL 1; 3

THE BIG PICTURE: For nearly two hundred years Israel was ruled by judges. Some of the judges, sometimes, relied on God's strength and obeyed his word. Some of the judges, sometimes, didn't! Samuel was the last and best judge. He was also a priest. And he was also a prophet. Oh, and he also anointed Israel's first king. He did it all! He was an important leader. And, for the most part, he was a good and godly leader. He was a special man called by God to hear and declare God's word to God's people.

READING 1 • 1 SAMUEL 1:1–2, 10–11, 20
A Woman's Tears

What made Hannah cry and cry? Whom did she cry out to for help? What can we learn from her? Does God always give us what we ask for?

....

....

....

....

READING 2 • 1 SAMUEL 1:21–28
Dedicated to God

Once Samuel was old enough, Hannah gave him to the priest Eli to serve God in the holy temple. What are some ways today we can dedicate our family and ourselves to God?

....

....

....

....

READING 3 • 1 SAMUEL 3:1–10
The Word of the Lord

At first, who did Samuel think was speaking to him? Who was really speaking to him? Does God talk to us today the same way he spoke to Samuel?

....

....

....

....

READING 4 • 1 SAMUEL 3:19–21
The Prophet

God chose Samuel to speak his words to the people. And he did it, no matter how difficult the message. How should we respond to what God tells us in his word to do? Have you ever shared the word of God with others?

....

....

....

....

READING 5 • HEBREWS 1:1–2

Spoken to Us

What are some of the ways that God spoke to people in the Bible? Who is God's final Word to the world? What is so great about Jesus?

....

....

....

....

GOSPEL CONNECTION: God revealed himself through visions and dreams. But now God reveals himself to us through Jesus. We know what God is like, what he has done for us, and how we are to respond to him by looking at Jesus. And the surest way we know about Jesus is by the word of God in the Bible. We read the Bible, learn about Jesus, and share the good news about Jesus with others. It is so important to listen to whatever the word of God tells us to be and to do—and then to share it with others.

PRAYER: Teach us your word, O Lord, that we may know you, know ourselves, and know what to do. And help us to share that knowledge with others. Amen.

STORY 26

The Rise and Fall of King Saul

1 SAMUEL 8–15

THE BIG PICTURE: Saul wasn't a great king, because he wasn't always a good man. And he wasn't who God had in mind when he thought of the right king for Israel. This is why, when Israel demanded a king, the Lord said, "They have rejected me from being king over them" (1 Sam. 8:7). They wanted a king that was just like all the other nations': someone who would rule them in his own strength. They wanted a great king *instead* of our great God! Well, God gave them what they wanted. Yikes! But some day he would give them the perfect King to rule perfectly.

READING 1 • 1 SAMUEL 8:4–9
Give Us a King!

Why did the Israelites want a king other than God? What did God think of the idea? Has there ever been a time you listened to the foolish crowd, or small group of friends, and made a decision that you knew was against God's will?

....

....

....

READING 2 • 1 SAMUEL 9:1–2; 13:1–4

Long Live the King!

Why did Israel choose Saul as its king? What should we look for in a godly leader? Do good leaders make a big difference to a nation? How so?

READING 3 • 1 SAMUEL 13:8–14

Not Keeping God's Command

It didn't take long for *tall* Saul to break a *big* rule. How did he sin? Whom was he trying to please with his choice? What are some ways we might feel tempted to please others instead of God?

READING 4 • 1 SAMUEL 15:10–11, 26–28

Saul Rejected as King

Because Saul "rejected the word of the Lord" over and over, the Lord finally "rejected" him "from being king over Israel" (15:26). Did Saul's rejection of God and God's rejection of Saul stop God's good plan for a future king? Do you know the name of the king who would rule Israel after Saul? Do you know the name of that king's King?

READING 5 • ISAIAH 53:1–6

No Beauty That We Should Desire Him

God gave Israel the king it wanted. Saul was a "handsome young man" and "was taller" than anyone in all of Israel (1 Sam. 9:2). He was also a mighty warrior. How is Jesus different? What difference does it make to us?

GOSPEL CONNECTION: God takes rebellious acts and brings about good through them. This is the story of the cross, isn't it? Jesus is born as the King of the Jews, but his own people reject, mock, and crucify him. But that rejection brings about God's good plan. Jesus dies and rebellious sinners are forgiven. Jesus dies and new life comes to spiritually dead people. Jesus dies and he is crowned King: "God has highly exalted him and bestowed on him the name that is above every name" (Phil. 2:9). Only God could take something as bad as Jesus's death and make it so good.

PRAYER: Forgive us, Lord, for trying to impress everyone except for you. Help us to do things your way—no matter what. Amen.

STORY 27

David Stands Tall

1 SAMUEL 16–17

THE BIG PICTURE: God "rejected" King Saul "from being king over Israel" because Saul "rejected the word of the LORD" (1 Sam. 15:26). In Saul's place, God raised up David. David was the youngest of eight brothers and was just a lowly shepherd, but he had three things going for him: God chose him, the Spirit of the LORD empowered him, and he had a heart that loved and trusted God. And when he walked in step with the Spirit, he ruled well and had great victories over God's enemies—even mighty men like the giant Goliath.

READING 1 • 1 SAMUEL 16:1, 6–13

Samuel Anoints David in Bethlehem

Why did Samuel think the oldest son would be the next king? Can we tell if people love and trust God by their appearance? Who is the only one that knows completely if we love God or not? And how does he know?

....

....

....

....

READING 2 • 1 SAMUEL 17:3–10

The Challenge

Why were all the Israelites afraid of Goliath? Would you be afraid? Be honest!

READING 3 • 1 SAMUEL 17:33–37

David Takes Up the Challenge

Why wasn't David afraid of Goliath? How can we be like David?

READING 4 • 1 SAMUEL 17:48–51

Who Wins?

How was David able to defeat the mighty Goliath? If we are Christians, we have the Spirit just like David. How can the Spirit help us when we feel weak or afraid?

READING 5 • PHILIPPIANS 2:3–11

In Humility

What did David do to defeat Goliath? What did Jesus do to defeat sin, death, and Satan? How are we *not* like Jesus? How should we be like him?

....

....

....

....

GOSPEL CONNECTION: David's heart beat after God's heart. Even though he was just a humble shepherd boy, he completely trusted that God could defeat Israel's biggest enemy through him. He didn't need special armor, a strong shield, a bronze helmet, and a long sharp sword. He just needed God's wisdom and strength. And that's what God gave him. David's humility points forward to Jesus's humility. David's trust in God was great—it led him through a scary battle. But Jesus's trust in God was greater—it led him through death itself! And so Jesus accomplished the greatest victory because he had the greatest humility.

PRAYER: God, help us not to be afraid of our enemies, for you are with us and will never forsake us. Amen.

STORY 28

David Sins . . . and Repents

2 SAMUEL 11–12

THE BIG PICTURE: David was a good king. He ruled God's people with mercy, wisdom, and kindness. He won many battles. And he became rich and famous. But more than the money, fame, success, and power, he enjoyed God's presence and promises. God so loved David that he promised him a kingdom that would never come to an end: "Your throne shall be established forever" (2 Sam. 7:16). Did this mean that David was the perfect king? No. Did this mean that he never sinned? No! David committed some big sins, and David, like us, needed a great Savior to save him from his sins.

READING 1 • 2 SAMUEL 7:1–3, 8–13
God's Covenant with David

What did David want to do for God? What did God promise to do for David? How long did God promise David his throne would last? Was David going to live forever? Then how would this promise come true? This promise is one of the most important in the Bible. Try to memorize 2 Samuel 7:13.

....

....

....

READING 2 • 2 SAMUEL 11:2–5, 14–15, 26–27

Two Big Sins

Think back to the Ten Commandments. What two commandments did David break? What commands are you tempted to break? What do you do when you are tempted?

....

....

....

....

READING 3 • 2 SAMUEL 12:1–9

You Are the Man!

How did Nathan show David his sin?

....

....

....

....

READING 4 • 2 SAMUEL 12:12–13; PSALM 51:1–2

David's Response

How did David respond in 2 Samuel 12? How did God respond to David's prayer recorded in Psalm 51? Has your heart ever hurt after you sinned? What should we do when we know we have sinned? How does it feel to know that God forgives your sins when you come to him?

....

....

READING 5 • ROMANS 5:6–8

While Still Weak

How do verses 6 and 8 describe people? Is that how you think of people? How did God show his love for us? Romans 5:8 is another great verse to memorize! Take the time to do so.

GOSPEL CONNECTION: God promised King David that through him and through one of his children he would create a kingdom that would never end. What kind of a king would it take to rule that forever kingdom? The perfect King! That perfect King is Jesus. David was good some of the time; Jesus is perfect all the time. David committed some big-time sins; Jesus never committed any sins, not even one. David needed a Savior; Jesus is his Savior. Jesus died on the cross for sinners (Rom. 5:8)—like David and like us.

PRAYER: We are sinners too, O Lord. Have mercy on us. Forgive us. Restore us. Amen.

STORY 29

The Wise and Foolish King

1 KINGS 3; 11

THE BIG PICTURE: Right before David died, he said to Solomon, "My son, you will sit on my throne and rule my kingdom. Walk in God's ways. Walk before God in faithfulness with all your heart" (see 1 Kings 1:17, 30; 2:3, 4). The prophet Nathan anointed the new king, and the people shouted, "Long live King Solomon!" (1:34). Would Solomon be a good king? A bad king? A wise king? A foolish king? Or maybe a good, bad, wise, and foolish king? And, most important of all, would he be the king to establish God's forever kingdom?

Watch Story 29 together

READING 1 • 1 KINGS 3:3–14

What Solomon Asked For

If God came to you and said, "I will give you whatever you ask from me," what would you ask for? When God gave Solomon the chance to ask for anything in the world, what did Solomon ask for? How did God answer his request? What can we learn from Solomon's example?

....

....

....

READING 2 • 1 KINGS 3:16–28

Wisdom to Do Justice

What a strange story, huh? How did Solomon use his wisdom? How do you seek to use the wisdom God has given you to help others?

....

....

....

....

READING 3 • 1 KINGS 10:1–10, 23

Wisdom (and Wealth!) beyond Measure

Who came to visit King Solomon? Did Solomon pass her test? Do you think all wise people are wealthy people? Do you think all wealthy people are wise?

....

....

....

....

READING 4 • 1 KINGS 11:1–6

Solomon Turns from the Lord

How did marrying so many women who were not part of God's people change Solomon's heart toward God? What happens when we stop following God with our whole hearts and worship people or things that are not worthy of our worship? What are some things that could take our focus off of God and lead us into sin? How can we make sure we keep loving God first?

....

....

....

....

READING 5 • MATTHEW 12:38–42

Greater Than Solomon

Solomon was known as a wise and powerful king, yet Jesus said he was greater than Solomon. In what ways do you think King Jesus is greater than King Solomon?

....

....

....

....

GOSPEL CONNECTION: Solomon was the wisest, richest, and most honored king in all of Israel's history. But, because of his foolishness and idolatry, he was not the king to establish David's forever kingdom. But Jesus was! He is the promised forever King! In Matthew 12:42 Jesus speaks of himself as being "greater than Solomon." Jesus is greater than Solomon in his wisdom, power, obedience, and glory. Solomon ruled Israel for only forty years, and his kingdom was split apart in the end. Jesus will rule all God's creation forever and establish his kingdom in peace.

PRAYER: O God, you are the only God, and we worship you alone. Keep our hearts steadfast all our days. Amen.

STORY 30

The Kingdom Cracks

1 KINGS 12

THE BIG PICTURE: King Saul was tall. King David was victorious. King Solomon was wise. Each king reigned for about forty years, and each king did some good things and some bad things. Some really bad things! Saul directly disobeyed God's order. David committed adultery and had Bathsheba's husband killed. Solomon married many pagan wives and started worshiping their gods. Bad. Very bad. As bad as bad gets. And every sin of theirs, like every sin of ours, had consequences. Saul died. David lost a baby. And Solomon lost his peaceful, rich, and unified kingdom.

READING 1 • 1 KINGS 12:3–14

King Rehoboam's First Folly

What two groups of people did Rehoboam go to for advice on how to rule God's people, and whom did he listen to? What would have been the wise thing to do? Do you ever listen to your friends' advice and not your parents' or teachers'? Is that wise? Is it always right to listen to older people?

....

....

....

READING 2 • 1 KINGS 12:16–20

The Kingdom Divided

What did the people of Israel think of Rehoboam's decision? What did they do to Adoram, the taskmaster, when he came to town? Do bad decisions have bad consequences? Is that true of your bad decisions too? What would you do if you lived under the rule of a bad leader?

READING 3 • 1 KINGS 12:25–33

More Golden Calves!

God's people were split in two. Ten tribes rebelled against Rehoboam and followed Jeroboam instead. But he ended up being even worse than Rehoboam. What did he do that was so bad? What story in the Bible does this remind you of?

READING 4 • 1 KINGS 11:30–35

Torn into Twelve

Was God surprised by the bad decisions of the bad kings and the bad consequences that followed? What does this show us about God?

READING 5 • MATTHEW 11:25–30

Best King Ever

Can you think of any king in the Old Testament that was perfect? How about in modern times? Why is Jesus the best King ever? How is he different from Jeroboam and Rehoboam?

GOSPEL CONNECTION: Because Jeroboam and Rehoboam didn't listen to God, God's people were divided. Would God's people ever find a good and wise king to lead them and bring them back together again? They would. Jesus is that King! He listened to God's voice. He walked where the Holy Spirit led him, even to death on a cross. But through his death, he showed God's mercy to God's people and brought God's divided people back into one body, his church. A good king is hard to find. In Jesus, we have the best King ever!

PRAYER: Dear God, too often we listen to the people who tell us what we want to hear, instead of listening to those with your wisdom. Keep us humble and make us holy. Amen.

STORY 31

Elijah Proves a Point

1 KINGS 18

THE BIG PICTURE: Of all the rotten rulers in Israel's history, King Ahab and his wife, Jezebel, may have been the evilest, nastiest, vilest, foulest, and cruelest. They were the worstest! (Okay, *worstest* isn't a word, but you get the idea.) This bad king and his bad wife did some bad things. They worshiped false gods and killed God's true prophets. These evil actions got God's attention. Our Lord hates idolatry and murder. What will God do about these evil, nasty, vile, wicked rulers who reject him and kill his prophets? Will the worstest win?

READING 1 • 1 KINGS 18:17–24

Elijah's Challenge

What did the evil king, Ahab, call the good prophet, Elijah? Why did you think he called him that? Who is the real "troubler of Israel," and why? Have you ever been called names for following God? How did that make you feel?

....

....

....

READING 2 • 1 KINGS 18:25–29

Heaven Is Silent

What did the prophets of the false god, Baal, do? What happened when they cried out to Baal? Are false gods real? Can they hear or act?

....

....

....

....

READING 3 • 1 KINGS 18:30–39

Fire from Heaven

What did Elijah do? Was his prayer answered? How? What did the big showdown between Elijah and the 850 prophets prove? Has God ever done something in your life that made you know that he is real and that he really cares for you?

....

....

....

....

READING 4 • 1 KINGS 18:1–6, 41–46

Rain from Heaven

After God's victory on Mount Carmel, how did he next provide for his people? Come up with a list of the ways God provides for you and your family.

....

....

....

....

READING 5 • MATTHEW 4:1–11

He Alone Is God

Who tempted Jesus? How did Jesus respond to the temptations? What lesson does he teach us in his response to the final temptation?

....

....

....

GOSPEL CONNECTION: After the Lord consumed Elijah's sacrifice, proving that he alone was the real God, he then judged the false prophets. God is holy and he judges evil. But God is also love, and he extends mercy and grace to those who trust in him and bow before him. After the great showdown God sent a great rain as a sign of his great care. In Jesus God shows both his holiness and his love. The same God who showed his great care to Israel when he sent the rain showed his care to us when he sent Jesus to die for all our sins.

PRAYER: God in heaven, you are the only God, and we worship you alone. Thank you for providing all we need. Amen.

STORY 32

Grime and Punishment

2 KINGS 5

THE BIG PICTURE: Before "Elijah went up by a whirlwind into heaven" (2 Kings 2:11), Elisha asked him for a "double portion" of his spirit (2:9). He wanted to speak God's messages and show God's power. That double portion was given to him! As a messenger, he instructed kings, rebuked enemies, and promised food for hungry people. And as a miracle worker he multiplied cooking supplies, de-poisoned a deadly stew, made an axe head float, and brought the dead back to life. And Elisha's story shows that God's message and power were not for Israel alone—Israel's God also blesses the nations!

READING 1 • 2 KINGS 5:1–4
A Mighty Man in Great Need

How is Naaman described? What is his problem? Who helps him, and is it surprising to you who helps him? What can we learn from her?

....

....

....

....

Story 32 • Grime and Punishment • 125

READING 2 • 2 KINGS 5:5–14

Wash and Be Clean

What did the prophet Elisha tell Naaman to do? At first, how did Naaman react to "the word of the man of God"? Do you think you would react the same way? Why was Naaman cured? Who cured him of the then uncurable disease of leprosy?

....

....

....

....

READING 3 • 2 KINGS 5:15–19a

Go in Peace

After he was cured, what did Naaman, the Syrian, say about Israel's God? Do you believe the same? Can people who are not part of the nation of Israel come to know and believe in the true and living God? Can you think of someone in your life who needs to hear that good news?

....

....

....

....

READING 4 • 2 KINGS 5:19b–27

Gehazi's Greed

Why didn't Elisha take the money that Naaman offered? What did his servant Gehazi do to get money from Naaman? Why did God punish Gehazi with leprosy?

READING 5 • EPHESIANS 2:4–9

The Gift

What was the best gift you ever received for Christmas or your birthday? What is the best gift that God gives us?

GOSPEL CONNECTION: Like Elisha (the prophet of God), Jesus (the Son of God) was powerful in words and works. One day, a leper approached Jesus, knelt before him, and begged, "Lord, if you will, you can make me clean" (Matt. 8:2). Jesus touched this untouchable man and answered, "I will; be clean" (Mark 1:41). The man was completely cleansed, just like Naaman was when he came out of the Jordan River. What a great picture of the gift of God's grace, grace that is for Israel, foreigners, lepers, our enemies—everyone!

PRAYER: Forgive us, Lord, when we are greedy. Be gracious to us when we don't value your gift of grace. Thank you for cleansing us from our sins. Amen.

STORY 33

The Boy Who Sought the Lord

2 CHRONICLES 34

THE BIG PICTURE: David was a good king, most of the time. Solomon too, some of the time. Josiah was a good king the whole time. His story begins with this sentence: "Josiah was eight years old when he began to reign" (2 Chron. 34:1). Eighteen? No, eight! Can you imagine ruling a kingdom when you were that young? What pressure! He was young, but God was with him. Josiah "reigned thirty-one years in Jerusalem" (34:1), the capital city, and "all his days [God's people] did not turn away from following the LORD, the God of their fathers" (34:33).

READING 1 • 2 CHRONICLES 34:1–7

The Boy King

How old was Josiah when he became king? Why was he such good king? What did he do? How should we be like Josiah?

....

....

....

READING 2 • 2 CHRONICLES 34:14–17

A Lost Treasure

What was the wonderful treasure that Hilkiah found in the temple? What gift do we have from the Lord that we can read? How can we treasure it?

....

....

....

....

READING 3 • 2 CHRONICLES 34:18–21

Reading the Book

How did Josiah respond when he heard "the Book of the Law" read? Would it have been true repentance if Josiah had only torn his clothes and been sad? What else is needed for true repentance?

....

....

....

....

READING 4 • 2 CHRONICLES 34:29–33

Everyone Listens to the Word

Did the people respond to God's word (called "the Book of the Covenant") the way Josiah did? How does having a good leader make a big difference? Who is someone in your life who helps you follow the Lord?

....

....

READING 5 • 2 CORINTHIANS 5:17–21

A Ministry of Reconciliation

Both Jesus and Josiah were great kings, but only Jesus is the perfect King. What was Jesus able to do on the cross because he was sinless, and why is this good news for you and me?

GOSPEL CONNECTION: Jesus is the completely good King. He never had to repent, because he is without sin. But Jesus's goodness would have done us no good unless he died for us to save us from our sin. And he did just that! For our sake God "made him to be sin who knew no sin, so that in him we might become the righteousness of God" (2 Cor. 5:21). Jesus destroyed our sin on the cross. When he returns, he will destroy all sin in the world. King Josiah smashed some idols; King Jesus will wipe out all idolatry and every evil.

PRAYER: God, what a gift you have given us in the Bible! Help us to know, love, and obey your word and to be grateful for our sinless Savior. Amen.

STORY 34

Promises Broken and Promises Kept

2 CHRONICLES 36

THE BIG PICTURE: When Josiah was king, God's people "did not turn away from following the LORD" (2 Chron. 34:33). They kept their side of the deal. They destroyed idols and worshiped God alone. They started to rebuild the temple and celebrate the Passover again. But after Josiah died, God's people went back to their usual pattern. There was hardly a promise they didn't break. God had promised in the days of Moses that if they broke their end of the covenant, they would be kicked out of the Promised Land. That was about to happen.

Watch Story 34 together

READING 1 • 2 CHRONICLES 36:5–10
Evil in the Sight of the Lord

Were Jehoiakim and Jehoiachin good or bad kings? How were they punished? Is it surprising that God used the Babylonians to punish God's covenant people?

....

....

....

READING 2 • 2 CHRONICLES 36:11–14
More Rebellion

What were some of the evil things Judah's leaders did? What are some ways we have been unfaithful to God? What should we do when we sin against God?

READING 3 • 2 CHRONICLES 36:15–21
Destruction and Exile

When God was patient, did his people change their hearts and put him first? What did God eventually do when the people refused to listen to his prophets and turn away from idols?

READING 4 • 2 CHRONICLES 36:22–23
God's Blessing through Persia's King

What did Cyrus decide to do? Why did he want to do that? Do you think God rules over all the leaders of the world—then and now?

READING 5 • EPHESIANS 1:3–10

Blessed in the Beloved

How many blessings do we have in Jesus? How are those blessings better than the rebuilt temple in Jerusalem?

GOSPEL CONNECTION: Is all hope lost? No! God would bring his people back, restore the city walls, and rebuild the holy temple. In Jesus, God has done more for us than all that. He gave us a King who showed how a good king should live by loving God and others. He suffered and died as God's King. Then he rose again from the grave and now reigns in power. One day he will return and take his people home with him. Together we will live forever in his perfect kingdom. We deserve curses instead of blessing. Instead, for all who are in Christ, we receive blessing after blessing.

PRAYER: O God, we deserve curses instead of blessing. Thank you for sending Jesus to bear the curse for us. Amen.

STORY 35

Walls and Worship

NEHEMIAH 6–8

THE BIG PICTURE: God raised up the Persian Empire to conquer the Babylonians. Then he "stirred up the spirit of Cyrus king of Persia" (2 Chron. 36:22) and made him decree that God's people should return to Jerusalem. "The LORD . . . has given me all the kingdoms of the earth," Cyrus wrote, "and he has charged me to build him a house at Jerusalem, which is in Judah" (36:23). Our very powerful God moved in the heart of a very powerful earthly king to send God's people home to rebuild the temple. And after the temple was built, God's people began another big building project—the walls of the city!

READING 1 • NEHEMIAH 6:1–9

Nehemiah Tries to Build a Wall

Why did people oppose what Nehemiah was doing? How did he respond? How should we respond when people oppose us when we are following God's word?

....

....

....

READING 2 • NEHEMIAH 7:1–4

The Wall Is Built!

The wall around Jerusalem is finally built and God's people have returned from exile. How wonderful! God's promise has been kept. Share something wonderful that God has done in your life.

....

....

....

....

READING 3 • NEHEMIAH 8:1–8

God's People Gathered around God's Word

What did Ezra and the Levites do? What did all the people do? What does this passage teach us about the right way to worship God?

....

....

....

....

READING 4 • NEHEMIAH 8:9–12

The Joy of the Lord Is Your Strength

Why did the people cry? Why did Israel's leaders tell the people not to cry? How can the joy that comes from God be our strength?

....

....

....

READING 5 • LUKE 4:16–21
Jesus Reads the Bible

What book of the Bible did Jesus read from? Whom did he say the reading was about? What did Jesus come to do?

....

....

....

....

GOSPEL CONNECTION: The days when Israel returned to Jerusalem, rebuilt the temple, and worshiped God were high points in Israel's history. But they weren't close to the highest. What could be better than a new temple? God's dwelling with us! What could be better than all God's people hearing and obeying God's word? Having God's law written on our hearts! When Jesus came, he did these better things. All who believe in Jesus are born again of the Holy Spirit and have new hearts that have God's law written on them. If the people in Nehemiah's day had reason to gather around God's word and worship, then we have all the more reason!

PRAYER: Thank you, God, for your holy word. Make us hungry to hear your word. Help us to rejoice in you as we worship. Amen.

STORY 36

More Than a Pretty Face

ESTHER 1–4

THE BIG PICTURE: The story of Esther is a great story! It starts with King Ahasuerus, the powerful king of Persia, throwing a big party that lasted a long time. He invited lots of people and showed them his riches. He also wanted to show off his beautiful wife, Vashti. But she refused to parade herself before all the people. This made the king so mad that he kicked her out of his court and got a new queen. Beautiful Esther! God raised up Esther, who was a Jew in exile, to save all of God's people.

READING 1 • ESTHER 2:15–23

Queen Esther

Why did Esther become queen? How did she save the king's life?

....

....

....

....

READING 2 • ESTHER 3:1–6, 13

Kill Them All!

Why didn't Mordecai, a Jew, bow before Haman? How did Haman respond to that?

....

....

....

....

READING 3 • ESTHER 4:1–4

Deeply Distressed

How did Mordecai and Esther respond to news of the letter that went out?

....

....

....

....

READING 4 • ESTHER 4:12–17

For Such a Time as This

When Esther heard about Haman's evil plan, what did she do? Why was it so brave to talk with the king? What can we learn from Esther?

....

....

....

....

READING 5 • ACTS 2:22–24; ROMANS 8:32

God's People Are Saved

King Ahasuerus listened to Esther and the queen was saved, along with all God's people. Jesus's enemies wanted him dead. How did God use their evil plan to save his people?

....

....

....

....

GOSPEL CONNECTION: God's people (like Esther) have always had enemies (like Haman). God's enemies hated Jesus too. Even his own people shouted, "Crucify him, crucify him!" (John 19:6). And the Roman soldiers did just that. But those enemies were no match for God. Just the opposite. Jesus's death was part of God's plan to save his people once and for all. After three days he rose from the dead and defeated our greatest enemies: sin, death, and the snake! One day, Jesus will come again to judge all who reject him and save those who take refuge in him. Find your refuge today in Jesus!

PRAYER: You are King over everything, O Lord, and work out everything just as you please. Thank you for the refuge we have in Jesus. Amen.

STORY 37

A Hard Life and a Good God

JOB 1

THE BIG PICTURE: During Solomon's day, Israel was at peace and their wisest people had time to think and write many poems, songs, and books. The books of Job, Proverbs, Ecclesiastes, and the Song of Solomon teach us wisdom. They teach us how to trust and honor God through lots of different experiences—hanging out with friends, falling in love, working, and suffering. The book of Job is about a man who suffered terribly and yet trusted and honored God through his sufferings. To learn about this incredible man, we need to go back to the time of Abraham, Isaac, and Jacob. Job lived back then, but his story is timeless!

READING 1 • JOB 1:1–5
The Man from the Land of Uz

How is Job described? Soon he would lose his possessions and children. So did being a good man keep him from suffering bad things? What can we learn from that?

READING 2 • JOB 1:6–12

Satan Wants to Test Job

Why does Satan think Job loves and follows God? Why do you think God allowed Satan to test Job? Do you think God should always protect us from Satan's testing and temptations in our lives?

READING 3 • JOB 1:13–22

A Very Bad Day

What bad things happened to Job? What did Satan think Job would do when these bad things happened? What did Job actually do instead? What should we do when bad things happen to us?

READING 4 • JOB 2:7–10

Another Very Bad Day

What happened to Job? How did he respond to his wife's bad advice? What can we learn from Job's responses to the suffering he experienced?

READING 5 • MATTHEW 4:1–11; 27:39–40, 50

The Tempted Son

Satan took away all the good things in Job's life, but Job kept trusting God. How did Satan tempt Jesus? How did Jesus respond? What are some ways that Satan might tempt us? How do we resist him when he tempts us?

GOSPEL CONNECTION: Job wasn't the only good man Satan tested. Jesus, the perfect man, was also tested. When Jesus was in the wilderness, Satan tempted him three times. He passed that big test ("Be gone, Satan!"), but it wouldn't be his last. When Jesus was being crucified, he was tempted to save himself and come down from the cross: "If you are the Son of God, come down from the cross" (Matt. 27:40). But Jesus resisted that temptation too. He chose to suffer and die for us. By staying on the cross, he passed the ultimate test. He not only showed he loved and trusted his Father but also, as the Snake Crusher, crushed Satan.

PRAYER: We praise you, Father, for sending your Son, the Snake Crusher. Amen.

STORY 38

Cover Your Mouth

JOB 38–42

THE BIG PICTURE: Satan tested Job's faithfulness to God. And Job passed the tests! A final test came when Job's friends came to visit him. They came to comfort him, but they ended up accusing him of sins he didn't commit. They thought the bad things that happened (the loss of his wealth and health) were because he did bad things. They were wrong. Bad things sometimes happen to good people. What was Job to do? His friends didn't help. And when he cried out to God, God was silent. Then, after many days, God finally spoke. Only then did Job realize that God alone is all-powerful, good, and wise.

READING 1 • JOB 38:1–11

God's Questions

For a long time, Job begged God to talk to him. Finally, he did. Why did God ask him these questions?

....

....

....

....

READING 2 • JOB 40:1–5; 42:1–6

Job's Answers

What do you admire about Job's responses to God?

....

....

....

....

READING 3 • JOB 42:7–9

A Sacrifice for Sin

What did God say about Job's friends? What did they have to do? Did they do it? What should we do when we say or do foolish things?

....

....

....

....

READING 4 • JOB 42:10–17

A Happy Ending

Job lost his health, wealth, and family, but what did he never lose? Even when Job was given back health, wealth, and family, what (or who!) do you think was his greatest treasure?

....

....

....

READING 5 • ROMANS 8:18, 31–39

Who Shall Separate Us?

Can anything separate us from the love of God in Jesus? How does that truth help you endure through suffering?

....

....

....

....

GOSPEL CONNECTION: As Christians, we will have very hard things happen to us like Jesus did. But we suffer "that we may also be glorified with him" (Rom. 8:17). Jesus died, but now he reigns as King in heaven. Like him, we will suffer and die. But one day we will join him in heaven. Suffering on earth; glories in heaven. And because we have this heavenly hope, we can remind ourselves of that future when things are hard. We can wait, knowing that "all things work together for good" for those whom God loves (8:28).

PRAYER: Life is hard, Lord. Help us to stay faithful to you. Also, give us the wisdom to hope in our future blessings. Amen.

STORY 39

The Lord Is My Shepherd

PSALM 23

THE BIG PICTURE: The book of Psalms contains sad songs about sad situations, longing songs that cry out for justice, and instructive songs that focus on living out God's wisdom. It has songs about saying sorry for sins, songs about God's forever kingdom, and songs that celebrate the coming of the promised King (the Christ!). Israel sang these songs when they gathered for worship. So did Jesus and his disciples. It became the church's first hymnbook. The church's favorite psalm throughout its long history has been Psalm 23—a beautiful, short poem about God's provision, protection, and presence.

Watch Story 39 together

READING 1 • PSALM 23:1-4

God as Our Shepherd

David, a shepherd and king, wrote Psalm 23. Psalm 23 begins, "The LORD is my shepherd." What does a shepherd do? What does that mean God does for us?

....

....

....

READING 2 • PSALM 23:5–6

God Is Our Dinner Host Too!

There are lots of comforting images in this beautiful poem. Which image from these verses, or verses 1–4, brings you the greatest comfort?

....

....

....

....

READING 3 • JOHN 10:14–18

I Am the Good Shepherd

How is Jesus the greatest shepherd of all? What did he do for us?

....

....

....

....

READING 4 • JOHN 10:27–28

His Forever

How do we know we are Jesus's "sheep"? What do you think it means to hear his voice? Once we are part of Jesus's sheepfold, is there any chance we will not dwell with him forever?

....

....

....

....

READING 5 • 1 CORINTHIANS 5:7; JOHN 1:29

Behold, the Lamb of God!

What animal was sacrificed at Passover? Who is the perfect Passover Lamb, sacrificed for our sins?

....

....

....

....

GOSPEL CONNECTION: David knew God's goodness and mercy all the days of his life, and now he dwells with the Lord forever. But while David was living on earth, he never met the spiritual shepherd who came from his family tree—Jesus! Jesus taught that he was a *shepherd* and that those who heard his voice would follow him like *sheep*. He also said, "I am the good shepherd . . .[who] lays down his life for the sheep" (John 10:11). Through Jesus's death, he takes away our sins so we can be forgiven. And because we are forgiven, we can dwell in the presence of God forever.

PRAYER: O Lord, you are our shepherd. We will follow you. May your loving kindness ever follow us. Amen.

STORY 40

The Beginning of Wisdom

PROVERBS 1

THE BIG PICTURE: In the Bible there is a whole book that has almost one thousand proverbs. It's called the book of Proverbs. God gave us the book of Proverbs to help us understand how to live a good and godly life. When we read through Proverbs, we can pray that God would give us his wisdom. The Bible tells us, "If any of you lacks wisdom, let him ask God . . . and it will be given him" (James 1:5). And this book of Proverbs tells us the most important secret to becoming wise: fearing the Lord.

  Watch Story 40 together

READING 1 • PROVERBS 1:1–6

To Know Wisdom

How would you explain wisdom to a friend? Is it just knowing a lot of stuff? Why would someone want to be wise instead of foolish? Why does God want us to be wise?

....

....

....

....

READING 2 • PROVERBS 1:7

The Beginning of Knowledge

Are we born wise? How do we become wise? What is the beginning of wisdom? What does it mean to fear God?

....

....

....

....

READING 3 • PROVERBS 1:8–19

Listen to the Right People

Whom should you listen to? Why? Whom shouldn't you listen to? Why?

....

....

....

....

READING 4 • JOB 28:20–28

Where Can Wisdom Be Found?

Where can wisdom be found? How do we grow in wisdom?

....

....

....

....

READING 5 • COLOSSIANS 2:1–5

Growing in Wisdom

Job 28 compares wisdom to a treasure. What are some things that you treasure? What do you think Paul means when he writes that in Jesus "are hidden all the treasures of wisdom and knowledge" (Col. 2:3)?

....

....

....

....

GOSPEL CONNECTION: Do you ever think of wisdom as a treasure? Something you would hunt for? Well, it is! And Jesus is where we can find it. In him "are hidden all the treasures of wisdom and knowledge" (Col. 2:3). So, if you want to become wise, go to Jesus. That means read the Bible, talk to him through prayer, and ask for his help to live wisely. It also means to put your faith in Jesus and what he has done for you on the cross. The Bible calls Jesus's death on the cross "the wisdom of God" (1 Cor. 1:24). So where can wisdom be found? In Jesus Christ and him crucified.

PRAYER: God, give us your wisdom—now and for all our days. Help us find in Jesus and his cross the wisdom we need. Amen.

STORY 41

What Isaiah Saw

ISAIAH 6

THE BIG PICTURE: When God had something important to say, he spoke through his prophets. They warned people that God was going to judge them for their sins. They held out hope of a time to come when God would make everything right. And they foretold a coming Deliverer, who would forgive sins, defeat enemies, and bring in God's perfect kingdom. Isaiah was one of God's prophets. He was called to do what is talked about above. It was an exciting job but also a tough one, because the people of Isaiah's day didn't want to listen to God's message to them through him.

Watch Story 41 together

READING 1 • ISAIAH 6:1–5

Holy, Holy, Holy

What do the seraphim repeat three times? Is their praise true of anyone other than God? Why was Isaiah terrified in the presence of a holy God? When you first think of God, what is the first thing that comes to mind—is it God's holiness?

....

....

....

READING 2 • ISAIAH 6:6–7
The Burning Coal

Who made the unclean prophet holy—cleansing him from all his sins? Who cleanses us from all our sins? Is it through an angel and a burning coal?

READING 3 • ISAIAH 6:8–10
Send Me

How did Isaiah respond to God's forgiveness? How should we respond? Did Isaiah have an easy mission? Do we?

READING 4 • ISAIAH 7:14; MATTHEW 1:18–23
Immanuel

How is the prophecy in Isaiah 7 fulfilled in Matthew 1? What does it mean for our family and church family that Jesus is "God with us"?

READING 5 • ISAIAH 53:6–8; ACTS 8:26–35

The Suffering Servant

Who is the suffering servant Isaiah spoke about? Do the Bible's fulfilled prophecies help you trust God's word more and better believe the true story about Jesus?

....

....

....

....

GOSPEL CONNECTION: How could Isaiah's sins be forgiven? What was the vision of the burning coal supposed to represent? The rest of the book of Isaiah fills in the picture. It tells us that the sign of his coming would be a virgin (Mary!) conceiving and bearing a son who would be known as "Immanuel" (Isa. 7:14), which means "God with us." It says that this deliverer would sit on David's throne and rule over a never-ending kingdom of peace (Isa. 9:7). And it speaks of a servant who would suffer so that our sins could be forgiven (Isaiah 53). Any guess who this could be?

PRAYER: Our holy, holy, holy God in heaven, help us to see you for who you are, that we might behold your holiness and experience your grace in Jesus. Amen.

STORY 42

Jeremiah against Everyone

JEREMIAH 1

THE BIG PICTURE: Do you know what is the biggest book in the Bible ("biggest" meaning "the most words")? Jeremiah. The prophet Jeremiah wrote over thirty-three thousand words! With his pen, Jeremiah shared some really good news. He wrote of God's faithfulness and the promise of his new covenant. But most of what he wrote and spoke about was God's coming judgment against God's unfaithful people. This was not the news God's people wanted to hear. Let's put it this way: Jeremiah didn't have a lot of friends. But God was his true and faithful friend. God's steadfast love sustained him throughout his tough life.

READING 1 • JEREMIAH 1:1–5
Called to Be a Prophet

Who did God call to be a prophet? When did God decide to call Jeremiah? Do you think God has a plan for your life?

....

....

....

....

READING 2 • JEREMIAH 1:6–10

I Am Only a Youth

Jeremiah was young when God called him to be a prophet, and he was afraid. What did he say to God? How did God comfort him? Do you think God can use you, even now, as part of his big plan for the world?

READING 3 • JEREMIAH 1:13–19

God's Judgment

How were God's people sinning against God? What was God going to do? Do you think the people would like what Jeremiah had to say? Would God protect his prophet?

READING 4 • JEREMIAH 31:31–34

The New Covenant

Despite all the bad news about judgment for disobedience, Jeremiah shared good news about a new covenant that would come. What was the good news?

READING 5 • LUKE 22:14–20

The New Covenant in Jesus's Blood

How did Jesus bring about the good news of the new covenant and rescue sinners from judgment? What did he do? How do we, as God's covenant community (the church), remember what he did?

GOSPEL CONNECTION: Everything Jeremiah spoke to the Israelites came true. He said the Babylonians would burn Jerusalem to ashes and capture God's people. He said God's people would be brought home after seventy years in exile. He said the mighty Babylonians would fall. And he spoke of a new covenant, a new promise, where God would remember his people's sins no more and write his law on their hearts. All those prophecies came true. And the last one came true because Jesus died and sent the Holy Spirit. Jesus rescued us from judgment and gave us, through the Spirit, new hearts to love, obey, and serve God.

PRAYER: Lord, thank you for the new covenant in Jesus. Give us the courage you gave to Jeremiah to obey your word and speak your truth—no matter what. Amen.

STORY 43

The Valley of Dry Bones

EZEKIEL 37

THE BIG PICTURE: Ezekiel wrote the book of Ezekiel *while* God's people were in exile in Babylon. His book describes six visions (or special dreams) he had over twenty years. The six visions talk about three big ideas: God's judgment on Israel, God's judgment on the other nations, and God's future blessings for Israel. The blessings are covered in the final chapters of his book. Chapter 37 records one of the most amazing visions in all the Bible: Ezekiel sees a valley of dry bones that come to life! Someday soon God would save his people and breathe new spiritual life into them.

READING 1 • EZEKIEL 37:1–6

Can These Bones Live?

What did Ezekiel see? Would you believe what the Lord told Ezekiel?

....

....

....

....

READING 2 • EZEKIEL 37:7–14
Raised from the Grave

How would you feel if you saw what Ezekiel saw? Scared? Excited? Amazed? Some other emotion? Did the bones' coming to life symbolize something good or bad for Israel?

....

....

....

....

READING 3 • EZEKIEL 37:15–21
Take Two Sticks

What did God promise to do for his people ("the house of Israel")? What did the joining of the two sticks represent or symbolize?

....

....

....

....

READING 4 • EZEKIEL 37:22–28
Great Promises

In these verses how many promises did God make to Israel? If you were Israel, which one would bring you the most hope?

....

....

....

....

READING 5 • EPHESIANS 2:1–5

You Were Dead

Without Jesus in our lives, how are we like those dry bones that Ezekiel saw? How do we come to life?

....

....

....

....

GOSPEL CONNECTION: Why did God give Ezekiel this strange vision? One reason was to teach Israel that as sure as the dead bones came to life, God would keep these promises. Another reason was to teach us about Jesus. The vision shows us how Jesus, the promised king like David, saves us. Like those dry bones, we are spiritually dead. But when God speaks his powerful word and sends his Holy Spirit, he breathes new life in us—just like he did for the bones. We were dead in our sins; God has made alive with Christ (see Eph. 2:5). Through faith in Jesus we are raised from death to life!

PRAYER: Thank you for the promise of your covenant and the power of your word. Give us life. Amen.

STORY 44

The Fiery Furnace

DANIEL 3

THE BIG PICTURE: God's people knew how they were supposed to honor God in Jerusalem with the temple nearby. But that was before the Babylonians came to Jerusalem, destroyed the temple, broke down the city walls, killed lots of people, and took the rest to live in Babylon. Far from home, their new king was the powerful Nebuchadnezzar. He had a long, hard-to-pronounce name, but that was the least of their problems. The Jews had to figure out how to honor God under a king who did not know God. Sometimes that was easy. But sometimes their faith was really tested.

READING 1 • DANIEL 3:1–7
The Golden Image

What did King Nebuchadnezzar command his subjects, and what does this command tell us about him? What does it tell us about the people who obeyed him?

....

....

....

....

READING 2 • DANIEL 3:8–15
Bow Down or Else!

Why were Shadrach, Meshach, and Abednego brought before the king? Did they do something bad or good?

....

....

....

....

READING 3 • DANIEL 3:16–23
Their Big No to the Bad King

Did Shadrach, Meshach, and Abednego say no to the king's command because they knew God would deliver them from the fiery furnace? What happened to them?

....

....

....

....

READING 4 • DANIEL 3:24–30
Amid the Fire

Did the three men die in the fiery furnace? Who saved them? What was the king's new decree?

....

....

....

READING 5 • JOHN 3:16–20

For God So Loved

Why did God send his Son? How should we respond to what Jesus did? What happens to those who don't believe?

....

....

....

....

GOSPEL CONNECTION: God sent the angel to deliver faithful Shadrach, Meshach, and Abednego from the furnace; God also sent us someone to deliver us—Jesus. These three men faced punishment because they followed God over the Babylonian king. By saving them, God showed to all that he is good to those who obey him. Our situation is different—we face punishment because in our sin we followed ourselves as kings over God. But God, in his great grace, still sent Jesus to deliver us! By saving us, God shows to all that he is *really* good to those who obey him, for now every person who follows Jesus will be rescued forever from death and the punishment we deserve.

PRAYER: Thank you, Father, for sending your Son to save us. And thank you for the example of Shadrach, Meshach, and Abednego. May we never put any earthly king or man-made commands before you. Amen.

STORY 45

Writing on the Wall

DANIEL 5

THE BIG PICTURE: At times Nebuchadnezzar was a mean ruler. He had Shadrach, Meshach, and Abednego tossed into a fiery furnace because they would not bow before his ridiculous golden idol. But other times Nebuchadnezzar did right. After God sent his angel to rescue the three men, Nebuchadnezzar said that the Lord was the true King. But his grandson, King Belshazzar, was different. Belshazzar was also a mean ruler, but unlike his granddad, he never learned to humble himself before the Lord of heaven. So God taught him a lesson he would never forget: God is against the proud.

Watch Story 45 together

READING 1 • DANIEL 5:1–4
A Great Feast

In these four verses King Belshazzar commits at least four sins. What do you think was his biggest sin?

....

....

....

....

READING 2 • DANIEL 5:5–9

Give Him a Hand!

How did the king react to the writing on the wall? Would you react the same way? Did his wise men offer a solution?

....

....

....

....

READING 3 • DANIEL 5:13–17

Daniel to the Rescue

Did Daniel agree to interpret the writing on the wall because he would receive great gifts? Why then did he help out the king? Who is the wisest person you know, and where do you think he or she received his or her wisdom?

....

....

....

....

READING 4 • DANIEL 5:18–30

Taken from Him

What happened to Belshazzar and his powerful kingdom? Why? Do you think that God still rules this way in the world today?

....

....

....

....

READING 5 • LUKE 5:1–11

Falling before Jesus

What is surprising about this story?

....

....

....

....

GOSPEL CONNECTION: The Bible says, "God opposes the proud but gives grace to the humble." One night Peter was fishing with fishermen friends, and they caught nothing. Jesus told them to go back out and try again. This time they caught so many fish their nets were breaking. When Peter saw what happened, "he fell down at Jesus' knees, saying, 'Depart from me, for I am a sinful man, O Lord'" (Luke 5:8). To fall before Jesus in humility is the right way to respond to King Jesus. That is why Jesus gave God's grace to Peter and called him to be an apostle. Jesus forgave a sinful man and sent him out to tell others the good news of God's grace. That is what he offers to us too—if we humble ourselves like Peter.

PRAYER: Forgive our pride, O Lord. Give us humble hearts before you. Amen.

STORY 46

The Miraculous Catnap

DANIEL 6

THE BIG PICTURE: As God predicted, the Medes and the Persians conquered the Babylonians after Belshazzar died. A new kingdom with a new king. The new king's name was Darius (which was much easier to pronounce). Darius's kingdom had 120 states with 120 governors. And to rule over all those governors, he picked three men—called "high officials." Daniel was one of them. He quickly became the king's favorite. In fact, Darius planned to make him rule over the whole kingdom. When the other two high officials found out, they were jealous and angry, and they determined to destroy Daniel.

  Watch Story 46 together

READING 1 • DANIEL 6:1–9
Tricking the King

Have you ever had someone try to get you in trouble? If so, how did you feel? What did you do? How did the two high officials trick the king and get Daniel in trouble?

....

....

....

READING 2 • DANIEL 6:10–15

Breaking a Bad Law

How did Daniel pray? Do you think we need to pray in the same way? What was brave about what Daniel did?

....

....

....

....

READING 3 • DANIEL 6:16–22

Into the Den of Lions

Are you afraid of big barking dogs? How about hungry lions? Did Daniel die when he was cast into the den of lions? Why not?

....

....

....

....

READING 4 • DANIEL 6:23–28

The King's Response

The king responded to Daniel's deliverance in at least four ways. Did he do anything unexpected?

....

....

....

READING 5 • ACTS 4:1–3, 18–20

On Trial

How did Peter and John reply to the leaders' command to stop preaching about Jesus? What would you do if the government said, "Whoever follows Jesus will be sent to prison"? Would you keep gathering with other Christians to worship Jesus? Praying? Telling others about Jesus?

....

....

....

....

GOSPEL CONNECTION: In the book of Hebrews, some people with great faith are listed. "Through faith," we are told, these heroes of faith "stopped the mouths of lions" and "quenched the power of fire" (Heb. 11:33–34). The author is writing about Daniel and his friends! Later in Hebrews, we are told that others, because of their faith, were mistreated, mocked, tortured, imprisoned, and killed. We also read that Jesus, who is called "the founder and perfecter of our faith, . . . endured the cross" (Heb. 12:2). If we are to keep the faith like Daniel, we need to follow Jesus, who trusted God even though it led to death. And just like God delivered Jesus by raising him from the dead, he will deliver us if we keep trusting him.

PRAYER: Give us faith, O God, to serve you alone, no matter who is watching. Amen.

STORY 47

A Marriage Made in Heaven

HOSEA 1–3

THE BIG PICTURE: The work of the prophets was hard work because they often preached an unpopular message to people who didn't want to hear. Some of the prophets had to warn God's people that God was going to judge them. Others had to tell people to turn away from sin and love God. But one prophet might have had the hardest assignment of all. Hosea! God told him to marry a bad woman who would be unfaithful in their marriage. The prophet's bad marriage was to symbolize how bad God's people had been to God.

READING 1 • HOSEA 1:2–9
Symbols of Sins

Do you know what your name means or why your parent gave you that name? How did the names of Hosea and Gomer's children symbolize God's relationship with Israel?

....

....

....

....

READING 2 • HOSEA 1:10–11; 3:5

Sand of the Sea

Have you ever tried to count all the sand at the beach? Of course not! What did God promise his people? What does that promise teach us about him?

....

....

....

....

READING 3 • HOSEA 2:16–23

Steadfast Love and Mercy

Do you remember the names of Hosea and Gomer's children? What does God say here that is so remarkable?

....

....

....

....

READING 4 • LUKE 23:32–43

Forgive Them

Does Jesus offer forgiveness to even really bad people, like criminals and those who crucified him? Do you think there is any sin that Jesus won't forgive?

....

....

....

READING 5 • REVELATION 21:1–4

A Bride Adorned

Who will be the church's husband forever? What does God promise to do for his people? What do you think when you think about heaven? What do you think it will be like?

....

....

....

....

GOSPEL CONNECTION: The short story of Hosea's love for Gomer is like the Biggest Story of God's love for us in Jesus Christ. We have broken the Ten Commandments. We deserve for God to show us no mercy. We deserve to be crushed along with the Snake. God should not call us his children. But instead, God does the unthinkable! He shows his love for us in that "while we were still sinners, Christ died for us" (Rom. 5:8). Through Jesus's blood (what a loving sacrifice!) we have been forgiven. We have a fresh start. He loves us as his children.

PRAYER: Thank you, God, for loving us so well when we were so unlovely. Amen.

STORY 48

Let Justice Roll Down

AMOS 5

THE BIG PICTURE: The prophet Micah wrote:

> [God] has told you, . . . what is good;
> and what does the LORD require of you
> but to do justice, and to love kindness,
> and to walk humbly with your God? (Mic. 6:8)

The prophet Amos couldn't agree more! Like most of the prophets, he tells God's people about God's gracious rescue plan that the Snake Crusher will usher in. But also like most of the prophets, he tells them that they are really big sinners who need to start thinking, speaking, and acting like God.

READING 1 • AMOS 5:1–3

Lamentation

Based on what is said in these verses, what do you think a "lamentation" is? Do you ever lament? Should you?

....

....

....

READING 2 • AMOS 5:4–6

Finding God

How is Israel to respond to all the bad things that are happening? More focused, what is the command that appears twice? Is that good advice for us too?

....

....

....

....

READING 3 • AMOS 5:11–15

Establishing Justice

"Injustice" is when people are treated in a way that isn't right and wouldn't please God. Like when someone is robbed or when a rich person can get out of trouble just because he is rich. In what ways are God's people participating in injustice? How do they (and we too) "establish justice" in our towns and cities?

....

....

....

....

READING 4 • AMOS 5:21–24

True Worship

Think about what we have read so far. Why does God not delight in their worship? What does true worship of our God involve? Have you ever gone to church on Sunday but treated someone badly right before or after the worship service? If so, what should you do?

READING 5 • MATTHEW 12:9–21

Justice to the Nations

What is your favorite miracle of Jesus? What miracles did he perform in this passage? How did his healing ministry bring God's justice to people?

GOSPEL CONNECTION: God promised that one day he would destroy evil and bring about a perfect world again. And he did so through Jesus, the Snake Crusher. When Jesus came to earth, he announced that the perfect kingdom of God had come near (Mark 1:14–15). And then Jesus showed us what that perfect kingdom looks like. The Snake Crusher lived as the prophets asked God's people to live. He always obeyed God. He was kind and loving. He was just and fair. He cared for the poor. He was humble. Jesus was so humble that he sacrificed his body on the cross so people like us—who aren't loving, just, or humble—might be part of God's perfect kingdom.

PRAYER: Forgive us, Lord, when we put others down to lift ourselves up. Give us grace to walk in justice and treat people fairly. Amen.

STORY 49

Famine and Feast

AMOS 8–9

THE BIG PICTURE: God uses all sorts of people to teach his word to his people. Amos was a prophet, but he was also a shepherd and farmer. He lived in Tekoa, a town on the border of Israel and Judah. The north was ruled by Jeroboam II, a really bad king. Under his leadership, God's people worshiped other gods, worked on the Sabbath, cheated people when they sold things, and ignored the poor. God gave Amos visions of his coming judgment for their bad behavior. And unlike the picture in the last lesson of a river of justice giving life to the land, these visions were not pretty.

READING 1 • AMOS 8:1–6
Trampling on the Needy

How should we treat people who are in need? How was Israel treating them? Did God like what was happening?

....

....

....

....

Story 49 • Famine and Feast • 193

READING 2 • AMOS 8:11–14; 9:8–10

The Days are Coming

What things will happen when God judges his people? What is the worst thing God promised to do? What would it be like to never hear from God again?

READING 3 • AMOS 8:9–10

That Dark Day

On the day of God's judgment, what will happen? Have you ever lost a loved one? How did it feel? How do you think Israel felt when God punished them with famine and exile?

READING 4 • AMOS 9:11–15

Restoration

What good news did Amos give about the future? Have you ever felt hopeless? What truths and promises from God's word can help you hope for a better future?

READING 5 • MATTHEW 27:45–50

A Dry Cry for a Dark Hour

Remember how Amos described the sky when he talked about God's judgment. What was the sky like when Jesus died on the cross? What do you think God was trying to show us? How can we escape God's judgment for our sin and receive his promised blessings?

GOSPEL CONNECTION: When Jesus was dying on the cross, "there was darkness over all the land" (Matt. 27:45). Yet that dark day was the brightest day for us! For, the moment the Snake Crusher died, Jesus provided the way to escape God's final judgment. How? He took the punishment we deserve for all our sins. He died in our place as the sky went dark with God's judgment. He died to save us from the final judgment. Then he rose and told his followers that he would be with them always. What a Savior! Let's run to him so we can escape the judgment we deserve.

PRAYER: Do not be silent, O God. Speak to us in your word and give us ears to hear. Amen.

STORY 50

Big Fish, Bigger Mercy

JONAH 1–4

THE BIG PICTURE: Lots of the prophets, like Amos and Ezekiel, were good and godly men. They were humble, obedient, and merciful. The prophet Jonah was different. God spoke to him and said, "Get up and go to Nineveh." Nineveh was a big city, but it was also a bad city. It was the home of the evil Assyrians. God told Jonah to go there and tell them that God had seen their evil deeds and was about to judge them for the terrible things they had done. But Jonah did the opposite. He ran "from the presence of the LORD" (Jonah 1:3) and the mission God gave him—until something miraculous happened!

READING 1 • JONAH 1:1–4, 12–16

A Great Storm

Why did God send the big storm? How did God save the sailors? How did they respond to God when he saved them?

....

....

....

....

READING 2 • JONAH 1:17–2:9

A Great Fish and Great Prayer

How did God save Jonah? In the belly of the big fish, did Jonah pout or pray? What do you like best about his prayer?

....

....

....

....

READING 3 • JONAH 2:10–3:10

Nineveh Shall Be Overthrown!

What happened when Jonah told the Ninevites that they were going to be judged because of their sins? Why did God save them? Why does God save anyone, including us?

....

....

....

....

READING 4 • JONAH 4:1–10

A Gracious God

What made Jonah mad? Glad? What should he (and we) learn from the lesson of the plant?

....

....

....

READING 5 • MATTHEW 12:38–42

The Sign of Jonah

What did the Pharisees ask Jesus to give them? What sign did Jesus say he would give them? How do Jesus's death and resurrection remind you of Jonah and the big fish? Have you ever asked God for special signs to prove he exists or loves you? If so, is that the best way to relate to God?

....

....

....

....

GOSPEL CONNECTION: On Friday Jesus died. That night (day one) and the whole day after (day two) his body was buried. Then, on day three, he rose from the grave! Jesus called his death and resurrection the "sign of Jonah." But Jesus didn't choose to connect his story with Jonah's simply because Jonah's story was, in some ways, like his. He chose the story because it was all about God's mercy for sinners who repent. Jesus's death and resurrection are the signs that proves he is the Son whom God sent to save us from our sins and the punishment of death. Anyone who trusts in Jesus—disobedient prophets or wicked enemies—can be saved.

PRAYER: God, teach us to love our enemies, just like Jesus died for us while we were your enemies. Amen.

STORY 51

A Change of Clothes

ZECHARIAH 3

THE BIG PICTURE: Israel was called to be holy—set apart from the other nations—based on *who* they worshiped (Yahweh alone) and *how* they worshiped (loving God and loving others). But God's people also needed holy priests to lead them, teach them, and model holiness for them. These priests would work in the temple and make sacrifices so God's people could be forgiven. They were very important, and so it was important they remained holy. It was so important that God designed special clothes for them. These special, clean clothes symbolized their important job. But there was one big problem with these priests. These "holy" men were often not very holy.

READING 1 • EXODUS 28:1–5
Holy Garments

What is your favorite outfit to wear? Aaron and the Levites (the priests) had to wear special clothes when they were serving in the temple in God's presence. How does Moses in Exodus describe them?

....

....

....

READING 2 • ZECHARIAH 3:1–5

Clothed by God

What was wrong with Joshua, the high priest? What did God do for Joshua? How are these verses a picture of what God does for us through Jesus, our great and perfectly holy high priest?

....

....

....

....

READING 3 • ZECHARIAH 3:6–10

A Wonderful Promise

Is this a positive or negative passage? Besides the answer to that simple question, there's lots of confusing language here. What is most confusing to you? What do we do when we don't understand something we read in the Bible?

....

....

....

....

READING 4 • HEBREWS 10:11–18

The Sacrifice for Sin

How is Jesus different than the priests who served under the old covenant? How should we respond to the good news expressed in this passage?

....

....

READING 5 • 1 PETER 1:13–16

Our Calling

Is it true or false that we are called to be holy because Jesus alone is holy and he paid for all our sins? What makes it hard to be holy? Who can we go to for help?

GOSPEL CONNECTION: The promised perfect high priest is called the "Branch" (Zech. 3:8) because he will come from King David's family tree. He might look like just one branch on a tree with lots of branches, but he will do what no high priest has ever done before: "Remove the sin of God's people in a single day" (see 3:9). Can you guess who the Branch might be? It's the Snake Crusher! When Jesus died on the cross, that very moment, on that one day in history, all our sins—past, present, and future—were paid for. Totally forgiven! Jesus took our stinky, filthy clothes and gave us his clean, perfect clothes.

PRAYER: Dear God, thank you for making us clean when we had made ourselves terribly dirty. Amen.

STORY 52

The Great and Awesome Day of the Lord

MALACHI 3–4

THE BIG PICTURE: This is the final lesson in the Old Testament! What are some of your favorite stories in the Old Testament? All these stories tell us something about the Snake Crusher, whom God would use to deliver us. He was the promised offspring of Abraham. He was the goat taken outside the camp. He was the Passover Lamb. He was the tabernacle that made a way for sinful people to be with a holy God. The Snake Crusher's entrance is getting closer and closer, clearer and clearer. But before he comes, we have one more prophet's voice to hear.

  Watch Story 52 together

READING 1 • MALACHI 3:1–5

Behold!

How many times did you hear the word "behold"? What is one thing God wants us to "behold"?

....

....

....

Story 52 • The Great and Awesome Day of the Lord • 205

READING 2 • MALACHI 3:6–7
Return to Me

What would happen if God's people turned back to God? Did they? What should we do if we have disobeyed God's word?

READING 3 • MALACHI 3:16–18
The Book of Remembrance

The prophet Malachi wrote about what would happen to God's people who were not obeying God. But he also shared about God's mercy. What will happen to the righteous, who are also called "those who feared the Lord"?

READING 4 • MALACHI 4:1–6
The Great and Awesome Day

What is the image God uses for his judgment of the wicked? How about the image he uses for his salvation of those who fear (trust) him? Who does he promise to send?

READING 5 • LUKE 3:1–6

Preparing the Way

What did John the Baptist say and do? Whom was he preparing the way for? How is Christian baptism related to John's baptism? What's the same? What's different? Have you been baptized?

GOSPEL CONNECTION: The New Testament tells us that John the Baptist is this messenger (an Elijah-like figure) who prepared the way for the Lord Jesus, Immanuel (God with us). Jesus is the good news God's people have been promised since the very beginning! He is the Snake Crusher that was promised to Eve. He is Abraham's offspring, bringing a blessing to all nations. He is the Branch from David's family tree, who rules as the forever King of the forever kingdom. Jesus is the Passover Lamb, the goat taken outside the camp, and the one who delivered from the fiery furnace.

PRAYER: We praise you, heavenly Father, for sending your Son to make atonement for our sins and to make us your people now and forever. Amen.

STORY 53

A New Baby and a New Beginning

MATTHEW 1

THE BIG PICTURE: What do we celebrate on Christmas? The birth of our country? No. The new year? No. When the groundhog sees its shadow? Come on, now. On Christmas we celebrate the birth of Jesus. You know that. But you may not know the strange way Matthew begins the story of Christmas. He starts with a long list of names, called a genealogy. *Genealogy* is just a fancy way of saying family tree. Why would he tell the story of Christmas with a genealogy? One reason would be to remind us that Jesus was a real person from a real family. For the other reason, let's read and find out.

READING 1 • MATTHEW 1:1; GENESIS 12:1–3

The Son of Abraham

Jesus is the Son of God, of course! But he is also called "the son of Abraham." What did God promise Abraham in Genesis 12? From what you know of Jesus, how do you think Jesus might have fulfilled that promise?

....

....

....

....

READING 2 • MATTHEW 1:2–6; 2 SAMUEL 7:12–13
The Son of David

Jesus is also called the son of David. What did God promise David in 2 Samuel 7? From what you know of Jesus, how do you think Jesus might have fulfilled that promise?

....

....

....

....

READING 3 • MATTHEW 1:7–17
Jesus's Family Tree

Lots of tough names to pronounce! Do you know anyone with a tough name to pronounce? Who is someone in that long list in Matthew whose name and story you know? From what you know of some of the people and stories, are all the people in Jesus's family tree people who always followed God's ways? What does that tell us about God and his plan?

....

....

....

READING 4 • MATTHEW 1:18–21
The Birth of Jesus Christ

Answer yes or no to the following three questions. First, does Matthew record the angel Gabriel's announcement to Mary? Second, does Matthew say that the Holy Spirit played an important part in Jesus's birth? Third, did Joseph obey what the angel said to him in a dream?

....

....

....

....

READING 5 • ISAIAH 7:10–14; MATTHEW 1:22–25

What's in a Name?

What are the two names given to the baby born to Mary? Why is Jesus called "Immanuel"?

....

....

....

....

GOSPEL CONNECTION: In the Old Testament we learned that the promised Savior would fulfill all God's promises, like the promises made to Eve and Abraham and David. The Savior will be the great King and the one who brings all God's family from all the nations under God's forever rule. Jesus is that promised Savior! That's what Matthew tells us. Jesus, like all of us, came from a family, and he was born at a time and place in history. But, unlike us, he was born of the virgin Mary and of the Holy Spirit. He is Immanuel—God with us! He is the promised Savior, who came to "save his people [even us!] from their sins" (1:21).

PRAYER: Father in heaven, we thank you for Christmas, for baby Jesus, and that you are with us. What great gifts! Amen.

STORY 54

Wise Men, Smart Move

MATTHEW 2

THE BIG PICTURE: Throughout the New Testament Jesus is given many names, like *Immanuel* (which means "God with us") and *Jesus* (which means "Yahweh saves"). Matthew also calls Jesus *the Christ*, because that word means "King." A long, long time ago, God promised that a king would come from the people of Israel who would be worshiped by people from every nation. Jesus is that King, and the story recorded in Matthew 2 gives us an early picture of what will one day be the world's biggest worship service. Wise men from the east followed a star a great distance to find the one they called "king of the Jews."

  Watch Story 54 together

READING 1 • MATTHEW 2:1–6
Where Is the Newborn King?

What is the brightest star you have ever seen? Why did the wise men follow the star from their homeland ("the east") to the Promised Land (the city of Jerusalem)?

....

....

....

READING 2 • MATTHEW 2:3–6

The Star of Bethlehem

Why did the wise men's question *trouble* (or deeply disturb) King Herod? Did he know the answer to their question? Who did? What is the answer? (Bonus question: What prophet predicted where Jesus would be born?)

....

....

....

....

READING 3 • MATTHEW 2:7–8, 16–18

Loud Lamentation

Did Herod tell the wise men the truth? What did Herod want to do with baby Jesus? Why do you think he wanted to do something that terrible? If you were one of Herod's soldiers and given this order, what would you do?

....

....

....

READING 4 • MATTHEW 2:9–12

And Behold, the Star

Did the wise men find Jesus in Bethlehem? How did they find him? How did they respond when they finally saw Jesus? How should we respond to him now?

....

....

READING 5 • MATTHEW 2:13–15, 19–23

The Great Escape

Why did the wise men and Mary, Joseph, and Jesus have to leave the Promised Land? Was this all part of God's plan? How do we know that?

GOSPEL CONNECTION: At the end of Matthew's Gospel Jesus says, "All authority in heaven and on earth has been given to me" (28:18). That's a lot of authority. Total power! Many powerful people, like King Herod, are not good people. But King Jesus is perfectly good. Unlike Herod, who lived in a stately palace, Jesus was born in a lowly stall. And unlike Herod, who sought to kill all his enemies, Jesus was born to die for his enemies—sinners like us. This is the good news of our good Savior. He is humble and gentle, yet great and powerful; he is King of kings, yet he came to seek and save the lost.

PRAYER: We love you, King Jesus. We give you all our gifts and worship you. Amen.

STORY 55

The Pointer and the Point

MATTHEW 3

THE BIG PICTURE: Centuries before Jesus was born, God promised to send a special prophet who he called "my messenger." This messenger's really important job would be to "prepare the way of the Lord" (Matt. 3:3). John the Baptist was the special messenger. He prepared the way for the Lord Jesus. He did this by baptizing people—including Jesus! He also did this by pointing people to Jesus. "He must increase, but I must decrease" (John 3:30) was John's mission statement. John knew Jesus was the long-awaited King from heaven. The one who would make everything right.

READING 1 • ISAIAH 40:1–5; MATTHEW 3:1–3

Preaching in the Wilderness

What was John's message? What does the word *repent* mean? Why should people repent? Can you think of someone you know who has repented and come to Jesus, perhaps someone who was just baptized in your church?

....

....

....

....

READING 2 • 2 KINGS 1:7–8; MATTHEW 3:4

Locusts and Wild Honey

Who did John dress like? What did he eat? Would you like to dress and eat like him? Why do you think he dressed that way and had such a strange diet?

....

....

....

....

READING 3 • MATTHEW 3:5–10

Two Responses

How did most of the people who lived in the city of Jerusalem and the surrounding area respond to John and his message? How did John respond when he saw the religious leaders—the Pharisees and Sadducees? Why did he respond this way to them and not anyone else? Does what he said to them scare you? How should we respond to John's message?

....

....

....

....

READING 4 • MATTHEW 3:11–12

Baptized with the Holy Spirit and Fire

Why was John called "the Baptist"? What does water baptism signify or mean? For example, drawing a heart on a birthday card *signifies* love; it *means* you love someone. John calls Jesus "he who is coming after me." How is Jesus's baptism different than John's?

READING 5 • MATTHEW 3:13–17

The Baptism of God's Beloved Son

Jesus is sinless. He never sinned—ever! He never will sin—forever! Here's a tough question: If John baptized people as a sign that they repented and that their sins were forgiven, then why did John baptize Jesus? What does Jesus's baptism teach us about who he is and what he came to do?

GOSPEL CONNECTION: John's baptism was a sign people were repenting and a sign that God was cleansing. But even John's baptism was a pointer. John said, "I baptize you with water, but he who is mightier than I . . . will baptize you with the Holy Spirit" (Luke 3:16). Sinners like us don't just need water. We need our sinful, dead souls to have life breathed into them by the Holy Spirit. John the Baptist couldn't make that happen. Only Jesus could. And the way Jesus made it happen was by dying on the cross for our sin. With our sin paid for in full, God could now pour his Spirit on us. And that's exactly what happens for anyone who trusts Jesus. God gives us his Spirit and makes us alive! What a baptism!

PRAYER: Father, send your Spirit to help us repent and believe in your Son. Amen.

STORY 56

The Sin That Wasn't

MATTHEW 4

THE BIG PICTURE: "All the promises of God find their Yes" in Jesus (2 Cor. 1:20). The Snake Crusher who was promised to Eve? Yes! The long-predicted son of Abraham who would bless the nations? Yes! The long-awaited Son of David who would rule an everlasting kingdom? Yes! Immanuel—God with us? Yes! Jesus is the fulfillment of lots of old prophecies and promises. But he is more! Jesus came and lived perfectly, unlike the people of Israel. For example, when Israel was tempted in the desert for forty years, they failed the test. Not so with Jesus. He resisted Satan's tough temptations.

READING 1 • EXODUS 16:1–4; MATTHEW 4:1–2

Into the Wilderness

Who led Jesus into the wilderness and what is surprising about that? Before the devil tempted Jesus, how was he like Israel? During the temptation, how was he *not* like Israel?

....

....

....

....

READING 2 • DEUTERONOMY 8:1–3; MATTHEW 4:3–4

The First Temptation

What is the devil called in Matthew 4:3? How did he tempt Jesus? Why did he tempt him in that way? How did Jesus respond? How does his response help you when you are tempted?

READING 3 • DEUTERONOMY 6:16; MATTHEW 4:5–7

The Second Temptation

Where did the devil tempt Jesus next? Why there? What did he call Jesus and why do you think he used that title? Both the devil in his temptation and Jesus in his response quoted from the Bible. Was the devil twisting Scripture? How did Jesus correct him? Have you ever been tempted by someone who twists the Bible to mean something it doesn't really mean?

READING 4 • MATTHEW 4:8–11; JAMES 4:7

The Third Temptation

The devil wanted Jesus to clamor for bread (like Israel had done), to put God to the test (like Israel had done), and to worship other gods (like Israel had also done). What command did Jesus give to Satan and did

Satan obey? How do the truths in James 4:7 help you to resist temptations? How does what Jesus said in Matthew 4:10 also help?

....

....

....

....

READING 5 • MATTHEW 27:39–50
Temptation at the Cross

Three times the Son of God was tempted; three times he passed the test. The third test, however, wasn't Jesus's last test. His final temptation happened moments before he died. Who tempted Jesus at the cross? How did they tempt him? How did he respond?

....

....

....

....

GOSPEL CONNECTION: People who walked by him, as he was suffering on the cross, said to him, "If you are the Son of God, come down from the cross" (Matt. 27:40). Imagine how tempting that must have been. Jesus, the powerful Son of God, could have pushed the nails out of his hands and feet, jumped to the ground, and saved himself from death. But he didn't! Why? Because he knew that the only way to save sinners was to die for sinners; the only way to offer the good news of salvation was to die. How wonderful that Jesus succeeded on the final test so now all who trust in him can be saved.

PRAYER: Dear God, thank you for your perfect Son, who passed the test for us. Give us your grace to resist the serpent when he tempts us. Amen.

STORY 57

The Sermon That Was

MATTHEW 5–7

THE BIG PICTURE: Matthew, Mark, Luke, and John all end with stories about Jesus's death and resurrection. But they also focus on Jesus's making disciples, healing the sick, casting out demons, caring for people's physical needs, and performing miracles that showed he was God's heaven-sent Son. This is why Jesus was called the Son of God, the Good Shepherd, the Lamb of God, and Lord. Jesus was also called Teacher, and that is because he was a teacher, or what we'd call a "preacher." Like your pastor, he regularly preached sermons. His most famous sermon was the Sermon on the Mount.

READING 1 • MATTHEW 5:1–12
Blessed

From what you know of mountains in the Bible, why do you think Jesus taught on a mountain? What is one thing that is surprising about Jesus's Beatitudes, the statements that all start with the word *blessed*? Reread Matthew 5:1–12, and, every time the word *blessed* is read, repeat it back and use your fingers to count how many times it is used.

....

....

....

READING 2 • MATTHEW 5:43–48
The Limits of Love

Our heavenly Father shows perfect love because he cares for both those who love him and those who don't. How are we to be like him? Is there someone in your life right now that you find difficult to love?

....

....

....

....

READING 3 • MATTHEW 6:9–13
The Lord's Prayer

Can you say from memory the Lord's Prayer? Try to! What is the name we should call God when we pray? What does this tell us about God? When you pray, what do you usually pray for? How does the Lord's Prayer teach us what to ask from God?

....

....

....

....

READING 4 • MATTHEW 6:19–24
Treasures in Heaven

Is having a lot money a good or bad thing? Do you think you'd be tempted to love money more than God if you were really rich or really poor? Why should we love and serve God, not love and serve money?

....

....

....

....

READING 5 • MATTHEW 7:21–29

What Authority!

When Jesus finished the Sermon on the Mount the crowd was amazed because "he was teaching them as one who had authority" (Matt. 7:29). What were some of the things that Jesus said about himself at the end of the Sermon that would have made the crowd think that?

....

....

....

....

GOSPEL CONNECTION: In the Sermon on the Mount Jesus says that in his kingdom, righteousness has to flow from our hearts. But there's a problem with that. It's one thing to expect us to do good things. We can try to do that. But how can I change my heart? How can I change who I am? Only God can do that! And that's exactly why Jesus came. To die for our sins and allow us to receive new hearts. When we trust Jesus, he changes our hearts. People who trust King Jesus are changed from within. Now that's the kind of people God wants in his kingdom—not self-righteous people who think they've done enough good works but meek people who mourn over their sin and love Jesus with all their hearts.

PRAYER: Dear God, help us listen to your word and learn from good preaching. Help us believe and obey. Amen.

STORY 58

Mr. Clean

MARK 1

THE BIG PICTURE: In the Old Testament we find an important list of rules that included what is clean or unclean (like a rat!), who might be clean or unclean (like a dead body), and how to get clean if you are unclean (the right way to wash). In the days of Jesus the most unclean person was a leper, who had an itchy, scratchy, sore, ugly skin disease that wouldn't go away. To keep other people from getting the terrible disease, lepers were to shout "Unclean, unclean" if they were coming close to people. Today's story is about how an unclean leper gets clean.

READING 1 • MARK 1:21–28
Another Unclean Man

Jesus began in public ministry on earth by traveling through many towns and villages in Galilee "proclaiming the gospel of God" (Mark 1:14). He also "healed many who were sick with various diseases, and cast out many *demons*" (1:34), also called *unclean spirits*. Before Jesus encounters the unclean leper, whom did Jesus meet in the synagogue? What did the man say do Jesus? Does he truly understand who Jesus is? What does Jesus do? What does this teach us about Jesus—who he is and what he came to do?

....

....

Story 58 • Mr. Clean • 229

READING 2 • MARK 1:40

The Unclean Leper's Prayer

With leprosy you lose feeling throughout your body, so you can't feel if you cut yourself or something bit you. You also scratch off parts of your body because you can't feel. This made lepers look ugly. They had sores on their skin, and they had parts of their limbs and faces missing. And people wouldn't get close to them. How would you feel if you had a terrible disease like that? What are some lessons we can learn from how, or the way, the leper approached Jesus?

READING 3 • MARK 1:41–42

Jesus Touched Him!

Before Jesus touched this unclean man (yikes and wow!), how did he *feel* toward the leper? What does that emotion tell us about our Savior? What did Jesus say and do next? What happened? Now, how does that make you feel?

READING 4 • MARK 1:43–45

See That You Say Nothing

Why did Jesus tell the leper to be quiet about the miracle? Did the leper obey? Is what he did good or bad? What would you do if you were him?

....

....

....

....

READING 5 • 2 CORINTHIANS 5:21

The Sinless Savior Became Sin

What does this verse teach us about what Jesus did on the cross? How should we respond to his sacrifice?

....

....

....

....

GOSPEL CONNECTION: Why did Jesus touch the leper when he healed him? Did Jesus need to do that? No. Sometimes he healed people just by saying a word. Plus, the moment Jesus touched the leper, according to the laws in the Old Testament, he should have become unclean. Ah, but that's just it. Here's the bigger miracle! Because Jesus is perfectly holy, he didn't become unclean the moment he touched the man. Rather, the man became perfectly clean. Jesus took away the man's uncleanness and gave him his cleanness. In that way, it's like a little picture of what Jesus would do on the cross—the biggest miracle of all!

PRAYER: Dear Jesus, we thank you for cleansing us of all our dirty sins on the cross. Amen.

STORY 59

Get Up!

MARK 2

THE BIG PICTURE: How does God forgive sins? In the Old Testament, God gave his people certain things they had to do. First, he asked his people to build him a tabernacle (later called the temple). In the temple was a holy place where our holy God would meet with his unholy people and they could seek forgiveness. Second, only certain people could go into this place on behalf of the rest of God's people. Only people from Aaron's family (from the tribe of Levi) could go into the holy place. Third, God instructed these men (called priests) to offer sacrifices for the sins of God's people in that holy place—that was how God forgave sins. When Jesus came to earth, he fulfilled all these rituals and made the temple system of priests and sacrifices obsolete. Now (and always) through him alone, God's people find forgiveness.

READING 1 • MARK 2:1–2

A Packed House

Have you ever met a famous person? Famous people are hard to get close to, because they usually have crowds around them. Jesus had become famous, and crowds surrounded him all the time. Was he famous for being a great singer, actor, or sports star? Why then was he so popular that people packed the house so "that there was no more room, not even at the door" (Mark 2:2)? What was he doing inside the house that day? What does what he was doing tell us about what he considered to be really important?

READING 2 • MARK 2:3–4
Jesus Saw Their Faith

Why were the friends of the paralyzed man trying to get to Jesus? What did they do to show their faith—that they believed that Jesus could heal him? Would you do that for a friend?

READING 3 • MARK 2:5–12
Which Is Easier?

What is surprising about what Jesus said to the paralytic, "Son, your sins are forgiven"? How did the scribes respond to that statement? In this story how did Jesus prove to everyone that he had the power to forgive sins?

READING 4 • MARK 2:12
Wow!

How did you feel when you are sick and someone gives you medicine that makes you feel better? How do you feel after you do something wrong, ask for forgiveness, and are forgiven? How do you think the paralyzed man felt when Jesus forgave his sin and healed his body? How did he react? How about everyone else—how did they react?

....

....

....

....

READING 5 • MARK 2:13–17

Jesus Calls Levi, a Big-Time Sinner

Why did Jesus call Levi, who was a big-time sinner? How did Levi respond both when Jesus called him and later that day? How should we respond to Jesus's call to follow him?

....

....

....

....

GOSPEL CONNECTION: Jesus called Levi to leave behind his sinful life and follow him. And when he accepted Jesus's invitation, he, like the paralyzed man, had his sins forgiven. Then he was so happy that he invited all his sinful friends to meet Jesus so they too could be forgiven. When the Pharisees heard about this, they didn't understand why Jesus would get together with such terrible people. They forgot what Jesus taught when he healed the paralyzed man. Jesus came to forgive *sinners*—that's the point. To experience the good news that Jesus has the power to forgive all sins, we must first recognize how much sinners like us need him.

PRAYER: Dear God, we believe in the forgiveness of sins through Jesus! Thank you for such love and mercy. Amen.

STORY 60

Follow the Leader

MARK 3

THE BIG PICTURE: Followers of Jesus are called *disciples*. When they began to follow him, Jesus's disciples also became part of Jesus's family. Last story we met Levi, the tax collector. Remember when Jesus called him and Levi left his old life and followed Jesus? He became a disciple. There are millions of disciples today, and there have been billions throughout history. But Jesus started with just a few disciples, and from those disciples Jesus chose a few men, whom he called *apostles*. When he said, "Follow me," they all left everything and followed him. Jesus became their leader, teacher, and friend.

READING 1 • MARK 3:7–12
A Great Crowd

Why did Jesus and his disciples get on the boat? What was Jesus doing that made people crowd around him? What is the most surprising thing about this passage?

....

....

....

READING 2 • GENESIS 35:22b–26; 49:28; MARK 3:13–15

The Calling of the Apostles

How many men did Jesus call? Why do you think he called twelve? The word *apostle* means "sent-one." Why did Jesus call them that? What did he send them out to do? As followers of Jesus, is our mission the same today?

READING 3 • MARK 3:16–19

The Apostles' Names

From memory, how many of names of the apostles do you know? Are you or anyone you know named after them? Besides their names, what other information does Mark share about a few of them? Why is that information important?

READING 4 • MARK 3:31–34

Here Are My Mother and My Brothers!

What is shocking about what Jesus says here? What does it mean to do God's will?

READING 5 • REVELATION 7:4–10

A Great Multitude

In the Old Testament God called the twelve tribes to follow him. In the Gospels Jesus called twelve men to follow him. Now that the gospel has spread throughout the world, how many people will be Jesus's disciples in heaven? Will they just be from Israel? What does that tell us about God and his love for the world? Do you know any other Christians from different countries?

GOSPEL CONNECTION: If you are a Christian, someone told you that God loved the world so much that he sent Jesus, that Jesus died for the sins of the world, and that now God calls everyone to turn from sin (repent), trust in Jesus (believe), and follow him (become a disciple). Like that person who shared the gospel with you, the apostles told people the good news about Jesus, and then the Holy Spirit worked in people's hearts so they would repent, believe, and follow. The good news about Jesus may be an old story now, but it is new every day for many people around the world. Jesus is still calling people everywhere to follow him. And those who follow him (no matter what language they speak) are part of the new people of God, children in God's one big family.

PRAYER: Dear Jesus, thank you for the gospel. Send your Spirit to help us to hear your call, get up, and follow you. Amen.

STORY 61

A Story about Soils

MARK 4

THE BIG PICTURE: Jesus told stories. He told simple, short stories about ordinary people and everyday events—a woman baking bread, fishermen casting their nets, a shepherd watching his sheep, a farmer sowing seed. These stories are called parables. Jesus often ended his parables, saying, "He who has ears to hear, let him hear" (Mark 4:9). He wanted people to listen and learn about the kingdom of God through his stories. But he knew that people needed his help to understand what he was saying. The parable of the soils, which we will listen to today, teaches us about the ways people either accept or reject Jesus's teachings. Listen up!

READING 1 • MARK 4:1–9, 33–34

Listen!

Pretend that you are part of the large crowd listening to this short story. What would you think Jesus is talking about? Would you ask, like the disciples did, for Jesus to explain the meaning of this parable?

....

....

....

READING 2 • MARK 4:3, 14

The Sower and the Seed

Who is the sower and what is the seed? What is a lesson we can learn from what the sower does?

READING 3 • MARK 4:4–7, 15–19

The Hard Path, Rocky Ground, and Killer Thorns

What happened to the seed thrown on the hard pathway? What about the seed thrown on rocky soil? What about seed thrown in the thorns? What do these three surfaces teach us about how people respond to the gospel? Have you ever shared the gospel with someone and they rejected what you shared about Jesus?

READING 4 • MARK 4:8, 20

The Good Soil

What happened to the seed thrown on the good soil? How much fruit did it produce? What does the parable teach us about how the gospel can take root in our hearts?

READING 5 • ISAIAH 6:9–10; MARK 4:10–13

The Purpose of Parables

Why did Jesus quote from the prophet Isaiah? What is surprising about what Jesus says here?

GOSPEL CONNECTION: Jesus taught that when we really believe the gospel, it changes us. Not always in one quick swoop over night, but steadily over a long time—like a farmer with his field. Does that mean that if we decide to be a Christian, we have to work really hard to be good enough for God's farm? No, if that were the case, none of us could be saved. Instead, we have to hold onto that gospel and let it go down deep into our hearts. The more we know the Jesus who died to rescue us from sin, the more we know the Father who sent his Son to rescue us, and the more God will bring change in our lives. Let's have good soil and hold tight to Jesus's gospel.

PRAYER: Dear God, please let our hearts be good soil that we might accept your word, walk in your ways, and live like a follower of Jesus all our days. Amen.

STORY 62

The Scary Boat Ride

MARK 4

THE BIG PICTURE: Jesus *said* and *did* a lot of things there. He prayed to his Father in heaven. He preached "repent and believe!" He forgave sins. He dined with tax collectors and sinners and shared the good news with them. He taught large crowds, often using parables—those simple, short (but symbolic!) stories. And he performed many miracles. Everything he said and did was on purpose. He was revealing his identity—who he was. He wanted his disciples to ask what they ask at the end of this story, "Who is Jesus?" We should ask the same question.

  Watch Story 62 together

READING 1 • MARK 1:34; MATTHEW 4:23–25
The Miracle Man

What are some of the miracles that the disciples had seen Jesus do? Of all the miracles that Jesus performed, what one would you have liked to see?

....
....
....
....

READING 2 • MARK 4:35–38

On the Boat

Have you ever been frightened on a boat, bus, car, or airplane? If so, what made you afraid? Why were the disciples afraid? Why was Jesus sleeping?

....

....

....

....

READING 3 • MARK 4:39

Peace! Be Still!

Did the wind and the waves obey Jesus? What does this miracle teach us about who Jesus is and what he came to do?

....

....

....

....

READING 4 • MARK 4:40

No Faith

Why do you think Jesus said his disciples showed no faith? What would it have looked like for them to have faith during the storm? When we encounter scary things, like the storm, what can we remember?

....

....

....

....

READING 5 • PSALM 107:29; MARK 4:41

Who Is Jesus?

Did the disciples ask the right question? What's the answer?

....

....

....

....

GOSPEL CONNECTION: Do you know what a boat's mast is? It is the two poles that stick up in the middle of the boat where sailors set the sails. If you've ever seen one, you may know it looks like a cross. While Mark doesn't tell us if the disciples' boat had a mast or not (it likely did), he is making a connection between the shape of this story and what happened to Jesus on the cross. On the waters Jesus saves his twelve disciples from drowning. A small salvation. But on the cross he saves all his disciples (including us) from the punishment of eternal death for our sins. Our big salvation!

PRAYER: We cry out to you, Jesus the Son of God, save us! Amen.

STORY 63

Send Us to the Pigs!

MARK 5

THE BIG PICTURE: After their scary boat ride, Jesus and the twelve arrived in the "country of the Gerasenes" (5:1), a Gentile region. The Jews viewed Gentiles as unclean people. And the most unclean person in that place was about to meet Jesus—"a man with an unclean spirit" (Mark 5:2). This man was possessed by demons and lived in a tomb that was filled with dead bodies. If that's not unclean enough, there was "a great herd of pigs . . . feeding there on the hillside" (5:11). Now you might think, "Piglets are so cute." But God's law clearly stated: "And the pig . . . is unclean to you" (Lev. 11:7). So this is one unclean scene! There's a demon-possessed Gentile living with dead bodies and pigs. Let's see how Jesus cleans up this unclean scene.

Watch Story 63 together

READING 1 • MARK 5:1–5

The Superstrong, Sad, and Mad Man

What is so sad about this man? Did people try to help him? Was anyone strong enough to save him? Have you ever seen a person, perhaps a homeless man, who seemed crazy and beyond receiving anyone's help?

....

....

READING 2 • MARK 5:6–10
Legion vs. the Lord

In the Roman army a legion was made up of six thousand soldiers. That's a lot of people and power! We will find out in the next verses we read, but who do you think will win the fight between our Lord Jesus (the "Son of the Most High God," Mark 5:7) and Legion (an army of evil angels)? What did Legion beg Jesus to do?

READING 3 • MARK 5:11–13
Send Us to the Pigs

So who won? How did Jesus rescue the demon-possessed man? Why do you think Jesus is able to be this powerful? What hard things do you need Jesus's power to help you with?

READING 4 • MARK 5:14–19
They Begged Jesus to Depart

The herdsmen (those who took care of the pigs) told a lot of people what happened. And as the news spread, many people came to see the once unclean scene. What was now different, or what has changed since the start of the story (5:1–5)? After this amazing miracle, did they receive Jesus with open arms? Why not?

....

....

....

....

READING 5 • MARK 5:18–20

What the Lord Has Done for You

What did the man do after Jesus rescued him? What has Jesus done for you that you can share with others?

....

....

....

....

GOSPEL CONNECTION: The Bible states that the "whole world lies in the power of the evil one" (1 John 5:19). The good news is that Jesus, the Snake Crusher, came to "destroy the works of the devil" (1 John 3:8). When the Lord defeated Legion, it was a picture of this power. But it was not until the cross that Satan's head was crushed. And it is not until Jesus's return—where he will toss the devil and demons into the "lake of fire" (Rev. 20:10)—that all evil will be destroyed. Until then we are in a spiritual battle. But, like the man in this story, we have been made clean and set free by Jesus. And like him we should tell our family and friends this good news of God's mercy. The Lord has done so much for us!

PRAYER: We are so glad, Jesus, that you are more powerful than the devil. Thank you for all that you have done for us! Amen.

STORY 64

A Sick Woman and a Sad Dad

MARK 5

THE BIG PICTURE: In the Old Testament, God gave his people a list of laws telling them what was clean and unclean. Certain animals were unclean. Bats and rats? Yes. Pigs? For sure. Squirrels? Them too. So, if someone ate an unclean animal, they became unclean. (And maybe sick too!) What else could make someone unclean? If someone touched a dead body, he was unclean. If someone was bleeding in a certain way, she was unclean. In Mark 5 Jesus does two remarkable things. He is touched by a bleeding woman, and he touches a dead body. Let's find out what happened to him and them.

Watch Story 64 together

READING 1 • MARK 5:21–24
A Sad Dad

Why was the dad sad? Who did he come to for help? Did he believe that Jesus had the power to help? What does Jairus's attitude and actions teach us about faith?

....

....

....

....

READING 2 • MARK 5:25–34

Who Touched Me?

What was the sick woman's problem? She too had faith that Jesus could help. Do you think what she did was right? What happened when she touched Jesus? What are some reasons you might go to Jesus?

....

....

....

....

READING 3 • MARK 5:35–36

Only Believe

At the beginning of the story Jairus believed that Jesus could heal his dying daughter. What is the really sad news he receives? What does Jesus tell him *not* to do, and what does he tell him to do? How does the ruler respond (you might have to read ahead to 5:38)? If you were in a similar situation, would you respond by following Jesus to see what he might do?

....

....

....

....

READING 4 • MARK 5:37–40

Into the House

How were the people reacting to the death of the little girl? Have you ever been to a funeral and seen people act like that? Did the people at the ruler's house believe what Jesus said?

READING 5 • MARK 5:41–43

Arise!

Why did Jesus touch the dead girl? What did he say to her? What happened? Are you afraid to die? If Jesus can raise us from the dead, do we need to fear death?

GOSPEL CONNECTION: Both the bleeding woman and Jairus were afraid. The woman feared she might never be healed; the man feared that his daughter would die. And sure enough, she did die! But both the woman and man had hope. They knew who Jesus was and believed he had the power to heal. What they learned, however, was that Jesus has more power than they could imagine. He has power to conquer even death! And because of this, Jesus's command to the ruler is a command we should hear and obey: "Do not fear, only believe" (Mark 5:36). We don't need to fear death, because Jesus has conquered death through his death. And he has given us certain hope that we will rise from the dead someday just as the girl did—and just as Jesus did two thousand years ago.

PRAYER: Lord Jesus, we thank you that you can save anyone—men and women, boys and girls, people that seem important and people that seem too sick to touch. Help us not to fear death. Amen.

STORY 65

The Voice Is Silenced

MARK 6

THE BIG PICTURE: Jesus said of John the Baptist, "Among those born of women there has arisen no one greater than John" (Matt. 11:11). Put differently, Jesus thought John was a pretty important person! He was important because he prepared the way for Jesus's arrival. He did so by announcing that everyone should repent and be baptized. He also told the evil king Herod that he should start living by God's rules, not his own. Over and over, he preached, "It is not right for you to divorce your wife and marry your brother's wife" (see Mark 6:17–18). How do you think Herod received that? What do you think might happen to John?

READING 1 • MARK 6:14–16

Is Jesus John the Baptist?

What are some of the amazing miracles Jesus performed? When Herod heard of Jesus's miraculous powers, who did he think Jesus was? Do you think he sounds crazy?

....

....

....

READING 2 • MARK 6:17–20

Chained

Why was John in Herod's prison? Do Herod and Herodias both want to kill John? Do you think John, knowing that a powerful person wanted him dead, was scared in prison? Would you be scared? What do you think gave him hope when he was scared (and can also give you hope)?

....

....

....

....

READING 3 • MARK 6:21–23

Herod's Birthday

Whom did Herod invite to his birthday party? Whom do you think Jesus would invite if he threw a party? After Herodias's daughter danced, what foolish promise did Herod make?

....

....

....

....

READING 4 • MARK 6:24–25

How Wicked!

What did the girl ask Herod to do? What did she mean by her request, "I want you to give me at once the head of John the Baptist on a platter" (6:25)? Why did she ask for that?

....

READING 5 • MARK 6:26–29

A Day of Death

Why was Herod sorry? What order did he give? Why were John's disciples sorry? How did what happened to John resemble what will happen to Jesus?

GOSPEL CONNECTION: Whenever people asked John the Baptist about who he was, he was quick to say he wasn't the promised king (see John 1:19–20). But he was like Jesus in one way—both of them died a cruel death. And with both of them, it seemed like evil had defeated good. But John the Baptist was right when he said that Jesus was far greater than him (see John 1:27, 30). Jesus rose up from the grave. Death and evil couldn't hold him. And the Bible ends with Jesus bringing in a perfect kingdom. In the end, good triumphs over evil. Jesus wins! His resurrection proves that. Hallelujah!

PRAYER: O Lord, we want to follow you, even when we know it might cost us everything. Give us faith to believe that with Jesus we will always win in the end. Amen.

STORY 66

The Happy Meal That Kept on Going

MARK 6

THE BIG PICTURE: One way throughout history that God has shown his love is by providing food. The garden of Eden was filled with the freshest fruits—mangoes, cherries, olives, almonds, and coconuts. Then, in the wilderness, God provided daily (and yummy!) bread from heaven. Finally, the Promised Land was called a land flowing with milk and honey. Imagine how delicious a honey milkshake would taste after wandering through the dry desert. So when God's people thought about the coming Christ, they pictured someone who would save them from sin, sickness, and even death and the devil. But they believed with the coming of the king would come some meals so satisfying they would fill you with joy—true happy meals!

READING 1 • MARK 6:30–34
Our Compassionate Christ

What's the longest you've ever gone without eating? When you are really hungry and tired, how do you act toward other people? When Jesus was tired and hungry, how did he act when he saw the crowd? Soon he would show his compassion (love) for the crowd by feeding them. How does he show his compassion here?

READING 2 • MARK 6:35–37
The Apostles' Attitude

What was the problem? What did Jesus ask the disciples to do? Did they believe what he asked them to do could be done?

READING 3 • MARK 6:38–44
Satisfied!

How much food was Jesus given to feed that many people? And what was he able to do with it that no one else could? Why?

READING 4 • EZEKIEL 34:15–16; PSALM 23
The Good Shepherd

How is Jesus like the good shepherd in these two Old Testament passages? Does it bring you comfort knowing Jesus knows, protects, and cares for you?

READING 5 • REVELATION 19:6–9

The Marriage Supper

Have you ever been to a wedding reception? If so, do you remember what food was served? When God's people are finally with Jesus (the Lamb) in heaven, what foods do you think will be there?

GOSPEL CONNECTION: When Jesus was tempted in the wilderness, he had no food for forty days. He was starving! And because of that, the Snake Crusher's answer to the serpent was surprising: "Man shall not live by bread alone, but by every word that comes from the mouth of God" (Matt. 4:4). Another time in Jesus's ministry (actually right after he fed these five thousand), he said something just as surprising. He said, "I am the bread of life; whoever comes to me shall not hunger, and whoever believes in me shall never thirst" (John 6:35). Wow, what a claim! Wow, what a wonderful promise. What do you think? Do you believe in Jesus? Have you come to him for everything you need, even eternal life?

PRAYER: You are amazing, Jesus! You are the bread of life! Feed us today our daily bread. Amen.

STORY 67

A Walk on the Water

MATTHEW 14

THE BIG PICTURE: Jesus needed physical rest. He needed spiritual rest too. To find it he told the fully fed crowds to return home. He also sent his apostles away. "Get on the boat," he instructed them, "and sail to the other side of the sea. I'll meet you there soon" (see Matt. 14:22–23). Then Jesus climbed a nearby mountain. Up on the high mountain he talked with his Father in heaven. As Jesus was praying, the sun started to set. So he hiked down the mountain. By the time he reached the shore, the twelve were on the boat "a long way from the land" (Matt. 14:24) and it was dark. Why was it taking them so long to reach the other shore? Another terrible storm! What happened? What did Jesus do next?

READING 1 • MATTHEW 14:22–23

On the Mountain

What did Jesus command his disciples to do? Why? Do you find it easier to pray when you are with people or by yourself

....

....

....

READING 2 • MATTHEW 14:23–27

It's a Ghost!

How did Jesus get from the top of the mountain to the disciples' boat on the stormy sea? Why did the disciples say "It is a ghost!"? What did Jesus say to them? How can we take comfort from Jesus's words when we are in difficult situations?

READING 3 • MATTHEW 14:28–31

Lord, Save Me

How did Peter show he believed it was Jesus and that Jesus had power over the wind and waves? Should we trust Jesus like that? What happened when Peter took his eyes off Jesus? When we have "little faith" (we doubt Jesus and his power) and we feel like we are about to drown, what should we do?

READING 4 • MATTHEW 14:32–33

The Right Response

How did the disciples know Jesus is the Son of God? Then how did they respond to him? How should we?

....

....

....

....

READING 5 • MATTHEW 27:50–54

Truly

What was said about Jesus at the foot of the cross? Was that the right response? It is one thing to call Jesus "the Son of God" after you see him walk on water, but it is another thing to say it after he died. Why do you think the centurion and others said what they said?

....

....

....

....

GOSPEL CONNECTION: Jesus showed that he was God's Son and our Savior in many ways. He multiplied bread and fish to feed over five thousand people. He healed every sickness imaginable. He raised the dead. And he walked on water and calmed storms. But his greatest demonstration of power was actually the one the Roman soldier saw when Jesus died on the cross. That showed the God's power because it's the way God saved us from our sins. Jesus's death was unlike any other. He died in our place. Let's us fall down before him and trust him completely, even when the waves seem big. He's strong enough to save us. Truly he is the Son of God!

PRAYER: Our Savior Jesus, help us to get out of the boat and trust in you, and keep us from drowning when we sometimes doubt. Amen.

STORY 68

A Dogged Faith

MARK 7

THE BIG PICTURE: Up until this point Jesus has spent all his time in the land of Israel, teaching and healing the Jews. One day, Jesus decided to go on a long journey "to the region of Tyre and Sidon" (Mark 7:24). That might not seem like a big deal to us, but it was back then. Tyre and Sidon were outside the land of Israel and *Gentiles* lived there. Even worse, these cities had a bad reputation. In the Old Testament these cities are where God's enemies—the Canaanites—live. So what is Jesus doing in enemy territory? Let's find out.

  Watch Story 68 together

READING 1 • MARK 7:1–9

Hypocrites

What upset the religious leaders (the Pharisees) from the holy city (Jerusalem)? Why was Jesus upset with them? Does God look only on the outside or the inside too?

....

....

....

....

READING 2 • MARK 7:24–26

A Big Problem

Like when Jesus went up on the mountain to get away from the crowd, he traveled all the way to the region of Tyre and Sidon because he "did not want anyone to know" (7:24) where he was. He needed a break, at the very least! Who interrupted him? Why? Do you think we bother Jesus when we come to him with our big problems?

READING 3 • MARK 7:27–28

Throw It to the Dogs

When Jesus tested the woman and said he came to heal the Jews and not the Gentiles (people who are not Jewish), how did she respond? Did this Gentile woman believe he came to save and heal the Gentiles too?

READING 4 • MARK 7:29–30

Great Faith

How do we know that the Gentile woman was right that Jesus came to save and heal the Gentiles too? Will Jesus save everyone who trusts in him?

READING 5 • ROMANS 1:1–7

God's Gospel

What did God promise in the "Scriptures" (referring to the Old Testament)? Was this promise of good news (the gospel) through Jesus for just the Jews or all the nations? What nation (or nationality) is your family? Are there people from any nation around the world that is too far for God's gospel to reach? Do you ever pray that God's gospel would reach all the nations?

GOSPEL CONNECTION: When the Bible talks about the gospel in Romans 1, it talks about those three things—*who* Jesus is ("the Son of God" and "our Lord"), *what* he has *done* ("resurrected from the dead"), and *what we receive* if we believe ("salvation"). But it also adds something else, a fourth important part of the gospel. It talks about *whom* the gospel is for. The wonderful answer is *everyone*! The good news about Jesus is for "all the nations." So, whether we are Jews or Gentiles, like this Gentile woman we can come to Jesus, bow before him, and receive mercy.

PRAYER: Thank you, Jesus, that we can feast at your table, when none of us even deserves crumbs off the floor. Amen.

STORY 69

Confessing Christ

MATTHEW 16

THE BIG PICTURE: One day Jesus and his disciples traveled to a place with a *big* name: Caesarea Philippi. It was a *big* name because it was named after some important people: the Roman Emperor (Caesar) and the Jewish ruler of that region (Herod Philip). But its importance didn't stop there. It had not one but two temples. One was the Temple of Augustus built to honor a Roman Emperor. The other was a temple to the Greek god, Pan. Not Peter Pan, just Pan—the god of the goats. Yep, the god of the goats! Anyway, it was in this *big* place—a place filled with worship of the wrong rulers and dead idols—that Jesus asked his disciples a *big* question.

READING 1 • DANIEL 7:13–14; MATTHEW 16:13–14

Son of Man

Jesus's favorite title for himself was "the Son of Man." Why do you think he liked that name? Who did people in Jesus's day think he was? Who do people in our world today think he is?

....

....

....

READING 2 • MATTHEW 16:15–17
Who Do You Say That I Am?

Did Peter give the right answer to Jesus's question? Did he get the right answer because he was super spiritual and super smart?

....

....

....

....

READING 3 • MATTHEW 16:21–23
Jesus's Mission

After Peter's correct confession, Jesus talked about how his church would be built and that no power from hell could stop its success. But he also said that first he must suffer and die. Did Peter like what Jesus said? Why was Peter so wrong; why was Jesus's death necessary?

....

....

....

....

READING 4 • MATTHEW 16:24
The Church's Mission

Is the church's mission totally different than Jesus's mission (i.e., he suffered, but we *don't* need to suffer)? What are some ways that Satan might tempt us to take the easy path and not obey Jesus's tough teaching?

....

....

READING 5 • MATTHEW 16:25-28

The Right Side of History

Will God's people win in the end? When will our final victory come? Who will have the better life in eternity—the man who lived for himself and gained many riches on earth or the poor man who lived for Jesus even though it meant sacrifices and even the loss of his job and home?

GOSPEL CONNECTION: The gospel clearly teaches that Jesus is the promised Messiah and the always-existing Son of God. We need to know *who* Jesus is like Peter did. But we also need to know *what* he came to do. Jesus came to suffer and die and rise. And through his suffering, death, and resurrection he brings the kingdom of heaven down to earth. First comes the cross, then comes the crown. If we trust in Jesus—that he came for us, suffered and died for us, and rose from the dead for us—we will live forever in his perfect kingdom. And Jesus calls us right now to pick up our cross and follow him.

PRAYER: Lord Jesus, help us to know who you really are. You are the Christ. You are God's Son. You died and rose again for the sins of the world. Amen.

STORY 70

Glory Mountain

MATTHEW 17

THE BIG PICTURE: Have you ever climbed a big hill? How did you feel when you reached the top? Were you out of breath? One day Jesus took Peter, James, and John on a long hike up a high mountain. We don't know if they were out of breath when they reached the top. What we do know is that they saw something awesome. Jesus was *transfigured*! That word means he was changed. But he wasn't transformed from a robot into a semitruck or a caterpillar into a butterfly. Jesus wasn't transformed into another thing. He stayed human; he just showed himself to be who he really was. God's glorious Son!

READING 1 • EXODUS 33:18–23
Please Show Me Your Glory

What did Moses ask for? How did God show his glory to Moses? Do you long to see God's glory in heaven forever and ever?

....

....

....

....

READING 2 • MATTHEW 17:1–2

A Light Show

What happened to Jesus? What did this transfiguration teach us about who he is?

_____

_____

_____

_____

READING 3 • MATTHEW 17:3–4

Peter's Bad Idea

If you saw what Peter, James, and John saw, how would you respond? Do you have any idea what was wrong with Peter's idea to build three little tents? (If not, wait for what God says next!)

_____

_____

_____

_____

READING 4 • MATTHEW 17:5

The Father's Voice

What two things did God say about his Son? What one thing did he tell his disciples to do? How do we obey that command ("Listen to him") today?

_____

_____

_____

READING 5 • MATTHEW 17:6–9
After the Transfiguration

How did the three disciples react to what they saw and heard? How did calm their fears? Why might Jesus have told them to be quiet about what they saw and heard until after his resurrection? Should we be quiet now about what we know about Jesus?

GOSPEL CONNECTION: Here, on Glory Mountain, we learn that Jesus is the *glorious* Son of God, who, like God the Father and Spirit, is perfectly holy. Now think about this. It would be surprising if a good man died for our sins. It would be amazing if a very important person—like a king—would take the punishment that we deserve. It, then, is truly astounding that Jesus—the King of glory—should lay down his life for us and die in our place. Peter, James, and John were confused, afraid, and surely stunned on the day Jesus took them atop the mountain. And while we should be amazed, we should not be fearful because we can take comfort in knowing Jesus died for us on Mount Calvary, a hill outside Jerusalem. He showed his glory to us by dying and rising again. What a glorious King!

PRAYER: Father in heaven, thank you for your Son and for showing us his glory. Amen.

STORY 71

The Kids Can Come Too

MARK 10

THE BIG PICTURE: Throughout the four Gospels we read about people coming to Jesus. A leper comes to him to be cured of his awful, yucky skin disease. Four men come to him to heal their paralyzed friend. Large crowds come to him to be cured of every type of sickness. One day, some parents brought their children to him. Why? Were the children sick? No. Were they hungry? No. Were they dying? No. They brought their children to Jesus so he might lay his loving hands on them and give them a special blessing. How beautiful! It is beautiful that these parents wanted that. It is beautiful that Jesus wanted that too. Not many powerful people want little children around. Little children can be noisy, messy, and, well, sometimes stinky. None of that bothered our Lord, who "took them in his arms and blessed them" (Mark 10:16).

READING 1 • MARK 10:13

Children Brought to Jesus

Why did parents want to bring their children to Jesus? Why didn't the disciples want them to? Even though Jesus is the glorious King, what is surprising about how he lived on earth and who he spent time around?

....

....

READING 2 • MARK 10:14–16
Let the Children Come to Me

What was Jesus's response to the disciples? What does it mean that the kingdom of God belongs to little children? Does Jesus welcome you to be part of God's kingdom?

READING 3 • MARK 10:17
What Must I Do?

Later we are told that the man who approached Jesus "had great possessions" (10:22). He was really rich! What is right about this rich man's question? What is wrong?

READING 4 • EXODUS 20:12–17; MARK 10:18–22
One Thing

Did the rich man think he was a good person who obeyed the Ten Commandments? How did Jesus test him to see if he really loved God and others more than his money? Did he pass the test? Are you tempted to love money more than God and others?

READING 5 • MARK 10:23–31
The Eye of the Needle

What name (it starts with a c) did Jesus call his disciples? Why do you think he used the word "children"? Is it hard for rich people to act like little children—humble and totally needing the help of others? Can having a lot of money be dangerous?

GOSPEL CONNECTION: Jesus doesn't test everyone like he did the rich man, but he does ask everyone to be totally dependent on him whether we are rich rulers or tiny children. The gospel is for everyone in the world. Because everyone in the world is small, helpless, and weak compared to God. What this rich ruler didn't realize is that no one can live with God forever until they realize they are as weak and helpless as toddlers. That's how God wants us to come to him. And when we do, he will take us in his arms and bless us.

PRAYER: Dear Jesus, we want to be a part of your family. Bless us and take care of us, we pray. Amen.

STORY 72

Who Is My Neighbor?

LUKE 10

THE BIG PICTURE: Remember how Jesus's disciples were upset that children were coming to Jesus? They thought Jesus was too busy, important, and powerful to waste his precious time with children. They misunderstood the King and his kingdom, so Jesus corrected them. The disciples weren't the only ones who misunderstood the King and his kingdom. They weren't the only ones Jesus needed to correct. There was also another group. But this second group was trickier and meaner than the disciples. They didn't like Jesus. They wanted him dead. Sometimes they'd ask him questions to get him into trouble. In today's chapter of the Bible they ask him one of those trick questions. But Jesus isn't tricked. Instead, he uses their question to correct their wrong views about his kingdom.

Watch Story 72 together

READING 1 • LEVITICUS 19:9–18

Love Your Neighbor

Do we naturally love ourselves? According to this passage, what are some ways we love our neighbor? What are other ways we can show love?

....

....

....

READING 2 • DEUTERONOMY 6:4–9

Listen Up, God's People!

This command is called the Shema because that is the first word in Hebrew ("hear" or "listen up!"). And to Israel to "hear" or "listen up" also meant to "obey." Should we love God with everything? Is it important that parents teach their children to know and obey the Shema?

....

....

....

....

READING 3 • LUKE 10:25–28

Jesus's Answer to the First Question

This expert in the Bible (called "a lawyer," someone who really knew the "Law" of Moses) tried to trick Jesus into giving the wrong answer. How did Jesus get him to answer the question? Do you think this man always and every second of every day loved God with everything? Do we always and every second of every day love God with everything?

....

....

....

....

READING 4 • LUKE 10:29–35

Jesus's Answer to the Second Question

Who didn't help the man? Who did? What is surprising about this story? How is Jesus like the Samaritan?

READING 5 • LUKE 10:36–37

Questioning His Questioner

The lawyer asked Jesus two questions. After the parable, Jesus asked his own question. What did he ask? How did the lawyer answer? Did he get the right answer? What is the point of the parable—to that man and to us too?

GOSPEL CONNECTION: Think again about what the Samaritan did in the parable, and then think about what Jesus has done for us. Like the Samaritan, Jesus came to the rescue. The Samaritan just crossed the road to do so; Jesus came all the way from heaven! The man who was beaten was rescued from dying; We were already dead in our sins when Jesus came for us. It cost the Samaritan some money to restore the dying man back to life; It cost Jesus his very life to restore our relationship with God. Jesus suffered for us. Jesus bled for us. Jesus died for us.

PRAYER: Jesus, thank you for your mercy. Help us to show mercy to others. Amen.

STORY 73

Lost and Found

LUKE 15

THE BIG PICTURE: Jesus told the parable of the good Samaritan to answer the lawyer's questions. And while the lawyer may have gotten an answer to his big question about living forever, there were still many more people with many more questions. There were also more people trying to catch Jesus doing something wrong—people who didn't like what Jesus was saying and doing. Jesus didn't like that they grumbled about God's grace or about spending time with people who were lost. And so, Jesus told more stories to show them why he came to be with sinners.

READING 1 • LUKE 15:1–7
The Lost Sheep

Why were the Pharisees unhappy with Jesus? How many times are the words "joy," "rejoice," or "rejoicing" used in Jesus's parable? What brings joy in heaven? Should we, like Jesus, share the gospel with all people, even really bad people?

....

....

....

READING 2 • LUKE 15:8–10

The Lost Coin

What is the same about this parable? What is different? Do both parables make the same point?

....

....

....

....

READING 3 • LUKE 15:11–16

The Lost Son

Like the two parables before it, the parable of the prodigal son is about something lost (the son) who is found. In what way was the son lost; put differently, what had he done to ruin his life? If you were so hungry, would you eat something disgusting—like pig's slop? What would you do if you were in the son's situation?

....

....

....

....

READING 4 • LUKE 15:17–24

Let's Celebrate!

What did the lost son decide to do? How did his father respond when his son returned home? What does this story teach us about our Father in heaven? If we have sinned against God, should we do what the lost son did—repent from our sins and return to God?

READING 5 • LUKE 15:25–32

He Was Lost, and Is Found

How did the older brother feel when his brother returned home and his father rejoiced? Would you have felt the same way? What did his father encourage him to do? How should we feel if God has found us?

GOSPEL CONNECTION: The older brother's thinking is common even today. It's easy to think we deserve God's salvation because we've done enough good things. We're not as bad as others (so we think). Jesus told the three "lost" parables to correct such thinking. All heaven rejoices when someone repents of his sins and returns to God—when the lost are found. That is why Jesus came and spent time with sinners. To seek and save the lost—like us. When we understand the true gospel, we rejoice that God came to rescue sinners of all kinds.

PRAYER: Amazing grace, how sweet the sound, that saved sinners like us. We once were lost but now are found, were blind but now we see. Amen.

STORY 74

Debts and Debtors

MATTHEW 18

THE BIG PICTURE: What should you do if someone steals something from you or tells a lie that gets you in trouble? One day Jesus taught his disciples what to do if someone sins against them. If a person admits his fault and asks for forgiveness, Christians should forgive. When Peter heard this teaching, he had a follow up question: "Lord, how often will my brother sin against me, and I forgive him? As many as seven times?" (Matt. 18:21). Jesus replied, "Not seven times, but seventy-seven times" (see 18:22). In other words, "Stop counting how many times someone sins against you. You are to forgive him every single time!" Jesus told a story to explain why.

READING 1 • MATTHEW 18:15–20

If Someone Sins against You

If someone sins against you, should you just look the other way or be really mad and mean? If the person who sins against you won't confess sin and ask for forgiveness, what should you do next?

....

....

....

READING 2 • MATTHEW 18:21–22

Seventy-Seven Times

Does Peter want a limit to how many times he should offer forgiveness to someone who sins against him? What does Jesus think about how often we should forgive those who ask us for forgiveness? Has anyone sinned against you in the same way a few times; if so, did you find it difficult to forgive? How many times will God forgive us when we sin against him?

....

....

....

....

READING 3 • MATTHEW 18:23–27

Jesus Tells Another Parable

A "debt" is when you own money. A "talent" was an amount of money. Ten thousand talents would have been the most money anyone in Jesus's day could imagine. Billions! Could the servant ever pay the king his debt? So what did the servant do? What did the king do? What does this part of the parable teach us?

....

....

....

READING 4 • MATTHEW 18:28–30

The Unmerciful Servant

How much money did the second servant owe the first? What should he have done when the second servant asked for time to pay his debt? What did he do instead and what was wrong with what he did?

READING 5 • MATTHEW 18:31–35

Forgive from the Heart

What did the king say and do to punish the first servant? What lesson is God trying to teach us?

GOSPEL CONNECTION: Our trespasses or sins are like debts we owe God. Our debt is as massive as the first servant in the parable. We owe God ten billion dollars. So what are we to do? *We can't do anything* to earn our salvation. But thankfully *God has done something* about our debt problem. He sent Jesus to pay it all. Jesus gave his "life as a ransom" (Matt. 20:28), a full payment. We, through faith, can accept that good news and have all our sins forgiven! And because God (like the king in the parable) has forgiven our many sins (like the first servant's debts), so we should forgive others (like the second servant's much-smaller debt) when they sin against us. The forgiven must be forgiving!

PRAYER: Father in heaven, all our sins have been forgiven because of Jesus. Help us to treat others like you have treated us. Amen.

STORY 75

Grumbles and Grace

MATTHEW 20

THE BIG PICTURE: Grace is God's kindness toward those who deserve punishment. So, let's think of some examples of grace throughout the Biggest Story. When God forgave King David's awful sins, that's grace. When Jesus called the tax collector Matthew to follow him, that's grace. When the father in Jesus's parable of the prodigal son welcomed his son home, forgave all his sins, and threw a big party to celebrate his son's return, that's grace. That's amazing grace! In Matthew 20 we learn more about God's amazing grace. It's another parable, one usually called the parable of the laborers (or workers) in the vineyard. By God's grace let's listen and learn!

READING 1 • MATTHEW 20:1–2

The Kingdom Is Like . . .

A "denarius," a small coin, was a typical day's wages for work. In this parable, what did the master hire the laborers to do? Did they agree to receive one denarius for their work?

....

....

....

READING 2 • MATTHEW 20:3–7

More Workers Hired

The "third hour" is nine in the morning. What is the sixth hour? The eleventh? Do you think the workers who were hired in the early hours of the day will get paid more than the workers who started at the end of the day? Should they get paid more?

....

....

....

....

READING 3 • MATTHEW 20:8–12

Wait a Minute!

Do you think you would have been upset too? If so, why?

....

....

....

....

READING 4 • MATTHEW 20:13–15

Don't Begrudge God's Generosity

How does Jesus say those workers should have responded? Why—what was the deal? Since God is the "master" not just in this story but the Master of heaven and earth and whatever is beyond, can he decide what he can do with us? Where did God show his greatest generosity to us? How should we respond to such generous grace?

....

READING 5 • MATTHEW 20:16

The First Last?

Do you normally want to be first or last in line—let's say for a yummy meal? In the story that Jesus told, who got paid first—those who started last and did the least or those who started first and did the most? What point was Jesus trying to make? Should we ever grumble about God's grace?

GOSPEL CONNECTION: Do you know what Jesus said right after he told this parable? He said, "Let us now journey to Jerusalem, for when we get there I will be delivered over to the Jewish religious leaders and they will condemn me to death. Then they will deliver me over to the Romans, and they will mock me and whip me and crucify me. But, on the third day, I will rise from the dead" (see Matt. 20:18–19). By going to the cross for us God gave us more than a hundred dollars. He gave us the most precious gift of eternal life through Jesus's death and resurrection. God gave us grace upon grace. How could we possibly grumble?

PRAYER: We know, our good God, that every good gift comes from you. We are sorry for complaining. Thank you for your grace. Amen.

STORY 76

Little Man, Big Faith

LUKE 19

THE BIG PICTURE: Remember how the first workers from parable of the vineyard grumbled when they learned the owner gave the workers who only worked one hour the same payment as those who worked all day? They lost sight of the generous heart of the boss, just like we lose sight of God's generous heart. None of us deserve his grace—no matter if we are first or last. We are all sinners deserving to be punished for our sins. That's what is fair! We don't want God to be "fair" in that way. Instead of being "fair" like that and punishing everyone, our just and generous God sent Jesus to save us. In Luke 19 we learn about one of those people. His name is Zacchaeus. No one in his town would have expected that Jesus would give him grace. But he did!

READING 1 • LUKE 19:1–4

Another Rich Man

What happened to the last rich man who approached Jesus—did he walk away happy or sad? To the Jews of Jesus's day a chief tax collector was the lowest of the low. So Zacchaeus was a big-time sinner! What is unusual about what Zacchaeus did that day? Would you run and climb a tree to see Jesus?

....

....

READING 2 • LUKE 19:5–6

Seeking Jesus

How did Zacchaeus respond to Jesus's command? Remember the parables of the lost sheep, coin, and son—how did Zacchaeus respond like those who found what was lost? Should we respond to God's grace with such joy too?

READING 3 • EXODUS 16:2–3; LUKE 19:7

Grumble, Grumble, Grumble

What did Israel do in the wilderness after God saved them from their slavery in Egypt? What has Jesus taught in some of his parables about grumbling about grace? What did the crowd grumble about?

READING 4 • LUKE 19:8

A Picture of True Repentance

When Zacchaeus received Jesus into his heart and home, he was a changed man. How did he express that change? If we receive Jesus, do we need to do exactly what Zacchaeus did? But what do we need to do to show that we love Jesus more than our sin?

....

....

....

READING 5 • LUKE 19:9–10

To Seek and Save the Lost

Salvation came to Zacchaeus because he, like Abraham, believed! If Jesus came to seek and save lost people—like chief tax collectors—do you think anyone is beyond the grasp of God's grace? Think of someone now who is so far from following God's ways. Pray for that person, knowing that God can do the impossible.

....

....

....

GOSPEL CONNECTION: The last line in the story, which is the most important, comes from Jesus. He says, "For the Son of Man came to seek and to save the lost" (Luke 19:10). Another way to say that is Jesus came to save sinners. Do you remember that Jesus said "it is easier for a camel to go through the eye of a needle than for a rich person to enter the kingdom of God" (18:25)? Zacchaeus is rich! So how did he get through the eye of the tiny sewing needle? Easy. Jesus pulled him through. He came to seek and save the lost—both rich and poor, short and tall. The next time you think about Zacchaeus, picture Jesus pulling a camel through the eye of a needle. Impossible? Not with God—all things are possible for him.

PRAYER: Thank you, Jesus, for seeking and saving us. Nothing is impossible for you! Amen.

STORY 77

The King Comes

LUKE 19

THE BIG PICTURE: If you were a great king and had lots of power, money, and servants, how would you decide to make your entrance into an important city, like Washington DC? Would you fly into the airport on a private jet and then take a big bullet-proof limousine through town? Back in Jesus's day, if the Roman Emperor rode into an important town, he would ride on a strong and beautiful horse with hundreds of guards surrounding him—holding banners, shields, and swords. When Jesus decided to make his entrance into Jerusalem, he did things differently. He came as the humble king, riding a small donkey.

READING 1 • ZECHARIAH 9:9; LUKE 19:28–34

The Lord Has Need of It

What was strange about Jesus's command? If you were the two men, would you have obeyed? Why do you think Jesus needed a colt, or wanted to have it?

....

....

....

READING 2 • LUKE 19:35–38

Blessed Is the King

What did the people say when they saw Jesus riding into Jerusalem? They called Jesus "King," but what kind of king did they expect—who would he be and what would he do? How was Jesus different than what they expected?

....

....

....

....

READING 3 • LUKE 19:39–40; PHILIPPIANS 2:3–8

Even the Stones Would Shout

When Jesus came to Jerusalem, did everyone recognize he was the promised King? Will everyone one day acknowledge humble King Jesus as the king of Kings?

....

....

....

....

READING 4 • LUKE 19:41–44

The Crying King

Why did Jesus weep when he saw in the distance the city of Jerusalem? Do you ever get sad when people you know reject Jesus?

....

....

READING 5 • REVELATION 19:11–16

The Rider on the White Horse

Who is the rider on the white horse? What is he called? How will Jesus's return to earth be different than the day he rode into Jerusalem on a colt? Does this picture of his return give you hope, and if so, why?

GOSPEL CONNECTION: Jesus wept the day he rode into Jerusalem because he knew what was about to happen. The crowds who shouted "Blessed is the King" (Luke 19:38) would only a few days later shout "Crucify, crucify him" (23:21). He wept because his own people would reject him as King. He also wept because he knew that in a few years, after the Romans crucified him, they would destroy the city. But is all hope lost? Of course not. We have the gospel—the good news! What is the good news? Jesus suffered and died. But then he rose from the dead. Now Jesus is crowned King and reigns in heaven. One day soon he will come again and enter earth (not just one city) in power and glory, riding on a white horse, with millions of mighty angels at his side. Then and there every knee will bow before him and confess that Jesus is *the* King.

PRAYER: You are the Savior, King Jesus! Give us life to sing and shout your praise. Amen.

STORY 78

Jesus Cleans House

MARK 11

THE BIG PICTURE: When Matthew wrote about Palm Sunday (the day King Jesus rode into Jerusalem), he taught that Jesus's riding on a colt fulfilled what the Old Testament prophet Zechariah said, "Behold, your king is coming to you, humble, and mounted . . . on a colt" (Matt. 21:5; Zech. 9:9). This verse tells us that Jesus's plan was God's plan. It also tells us we serve a humble king. Jesus was humble—and meek and mild and kind and gentle. But, when he needed to, he also showed his awesome power and righteous anger. "Righteous anger" is getting mad about things that upset God, things such as someone stealing food from the poor. The day after Palm Sunday, Jesus showed such anger. He cleansed God's holy house of the unholy.

READING 1 • MARK 11:12–14

Jesus Curses a Fig Tree

We will try to make sense of this short story later. For now, what doesn't make sense to you about what Jesus does?

....

....

....

Story 78 • Jesus Cleans House • 309

READING 2 • MARK 11:15–16

Jesus Cleanses the Temple

What was happening in the temple courts when Jesus entered? What was supposed to happen there? Jesus was angry that the temple court was full of cheaters and that there was no place for people from other nations to pray. Are those good reasons to be upset? When you get upset, do you always get upset for the right reasons?

READING 3 • JEREMIAH 7:8–11; MARK 11:17–18

A Den of Robbers

A den of robbers is the safe hideout that thieves return to. Even though they might be saying "We are safe," can God see them in their hideout? Will he someday judge what they did? If we say we are Christians, get baptized, and go to church and feel safe (God loves us) but we don't love God or others, should we say "We are safe" or should we repent?

READING 4 • MARK 11:19–24; GALATIANS 5:22–23

Have Faith!

Jesus was angry at the fig tree because it looked like it should have fruit but it didn't! Is Jesus happy when churches and people look great on the outside (have green leaves) but inside are not good at all (there is no fruit)? Tough question: How does what Jesus teach about faith ("Have faith in God," 11:22), prayer ("ask in prayer," 11:24), and forgiveness ("forgive" others, 11:25) relate to his cursing the fig tree and cleansing the temple? If we live by the Spirit, what fruit we will produce?

READING 5 • NUMBERS 28:16–25; JOHN 2:18–22

Destroy This Temple

What did Jesus say would be destroyed? What did he say would happen three days later? What was he talking about? How is Jesus like the temple? How is he better than the temple?

GOSPEL CONNECTION: Jesus talked about the "temple of his body" (John 2:21) and how it would be destroyed (he'd be killed on the cross) but raised up "in three days" (2:19). He also taught, another time, that he was "greater than the temple" (Matt. 12:6). What was he talking about? Jesus was teaching that he was the new and better temple. Think about it. Do we travel to Jerusalem to have our sins forgiven? No. We go to Jesus. Do we need to buy an animal and have it brought to the high priest? No. Jesus is our high priest. Do we need an animal to be sacrificed? No. Jesus is our sacrifice for sin. Jesus is greater than the temple because he is the only person that we need to go to for God's mercy. What incredibly good news!

PRAYER: God our Father, we don't want to just look like Christians. We want to be Jesus's true and faithful followers. Amen.

STORY 79

A Woman to Be Remembered

JOHN 12

THE BIG PICTURE: For special dinners guests would recline on their stomachs around a table and the food would be placed in the center. Everyone around the table would grab the food from the center, and their feet would stick out the back. As Martha was serving the guests, her sister Mary was listening to Jesus teach. He was likely teaching about what was about to happen to him in Jerusalem. He would suffer, die, and rise again. Mary was so moved by Jesus's teaching that she went to her room, grabbed something, came back, and ended up doing something that some people called a waste but Jesus called beautiful.

READING 1 • JOHN 12:1–2
Reclining at Table

What important Jewish feast were they about to celebrate? What amazing event just happened?

....

....

....

....

READING 2 • JOHN 11:32–44

Rewind to a Resurrection

When is the last time you cried? Why did you cry? Why was Mary crying? Why did Jesus weep too? What did Jesus do next? What do Jesus's tears and power teach us about him?

....

....

....

....

READING 3 • JOHN 12:3–6; MARK 14:4–7

A Beautiful Thing

What did Mary do while Jesus was reclining at the table? Why was Judas upset? What did Jesus think of what she did? Would you ever do something like Mary did?

....

....

....

....

READING 4 • JOHN 12:7–8; MARK 14:8–9

In Memory of Her

What did Mary's perfume prepare Jesus for? Mary's love for Jesus was costly (she dumped out an expensive jar of perfume), and people thought it was crazy, or at least wasteful! But Jesus thought it was both beautiful and memorable. What does what Jesus says teach us about what matters most to him?

READING 5 • 1 JOHN 4:7–11

No Greater Love

As much as Mary showed her love for Jesus, how does Jesus show his love for us? Because Jesus loved us, whom should we love?

GOSPEL CONNECTION: When Mary poured the perfume on Jesus's feet, he was still alive. But his death was coming soon, even if Mary didn't know it. Regardless, Mary loved Jesus so much that she wanted to give him the best she had. Jesus, however, knew he would die in a few days. And he saw her gift as preparing him for burial. He responded to her extravagant gift by saying she had done a beautiful thing. Anytime we worship Jesus, it is beautiful. He is worthy of the most extravagant, costly worship we can give. Her costly gift was given to the one who would give the costliest gift to us—his life. As we remember Mary's gift, may we remember how it points us towards Jesus's burial and death and his great love for us.

PRAYER: Lord, help us to love you and not worry about what others think. You are worth more than we can give. Amen.

STORY 80

A Meal for the Ages

MATTHEW 26

THE BIG PICTURE: One of the most important jobs God's people have is to remember. Jesus said that we should remember what Mary did when she anointed Jesus's body with expensive perfume. That special act symbolized his burial. In the Old Testament, God's people were supposed to remember the Passover, when God rescued them out of Egypt. Matthew 26 records the last time that Jesus celebrated the Passover feast with his disciples and where he said, "Take and eat," he said. "This is my body, which is given for you. Do this in remembrance of me" (see Matt. 26:26; Luke 22:19). He turned the Passover meal into a meal that would help Christians remember what he did for us.

READING 1 • MATTHEW 26:17–19

Preparation

What word (that starts with a *P*) is repeated three times? Why is that word important? Does anyone remember what happened in the book of Exodus at the first Passover? Put differently, why is the *Passover* called the *pass over*?

....

....

READING 2 • MATTHEW 26:20–25

Jesus's Sad Prediction

The Passover meal was a meal to celebrate the good news of God's deliverance. But what did Jesus say that would have made everyone sad? Why would anyone want to betray Jesus? Are you ever tempted to betray him?

READING 3 • EXODUS 12:14–20; MATTHEW 26:26

The Bread

Why did Jewish people eat unleavened bread at Passover? What did Jesus say at the Passover about the bread that would have been something totally new? What did he mean by the phrase "This is my body"?

READING 4 • EXODUS 12:21–27; MATTHEW 26:27–29

The Cup

For the Passover meal, what animal was killed and why? When Jesus talks about a sacrifice, does he talk about a lamb? Who is the new Passover sacrifice?

READING 5 • 1 CORINTHIANS 11:23–26

The New Covenant Meal

When Christians gather for the Lord's Supper or Communion, what do we eat and drink? Why? The Lord's Supper or Communion is also called the Eucharist because that Greek word means "to give thanks." When we eat the bread and drink the cup what should we be thankful for?

GOSPEL CONNECTION: Right before Mary anointed Jesus with perfume, he announced to his disciples, "The Passover is coming, and when it comes the Son of Man [Jesus!] will be delivered up to be crucified" (see Matt. 26:2). And right before Jesus was handed over to be crucified, he celebrated the Passover meal with his disciples. Why? He wanted them, and all Christians throughout all time, to make an important connection. Jesus is the perfect Passover Lamb, who was sacrificed for our sins. Our sins are *passed over* only because he died in our place! And like those Israelites in Egypt who believed what God said and took the lamb's blood and smeared it on their doorway, we believe that the blood of Jesus saves us now and that God will pass over us on judgment day.

PRAYER: Jesus, you are the Passover Lamb! Thank you for your sacrifice—the Lamb of God who takes away the sins of the world. May we always remember who you are and what you have done for us. Amen.

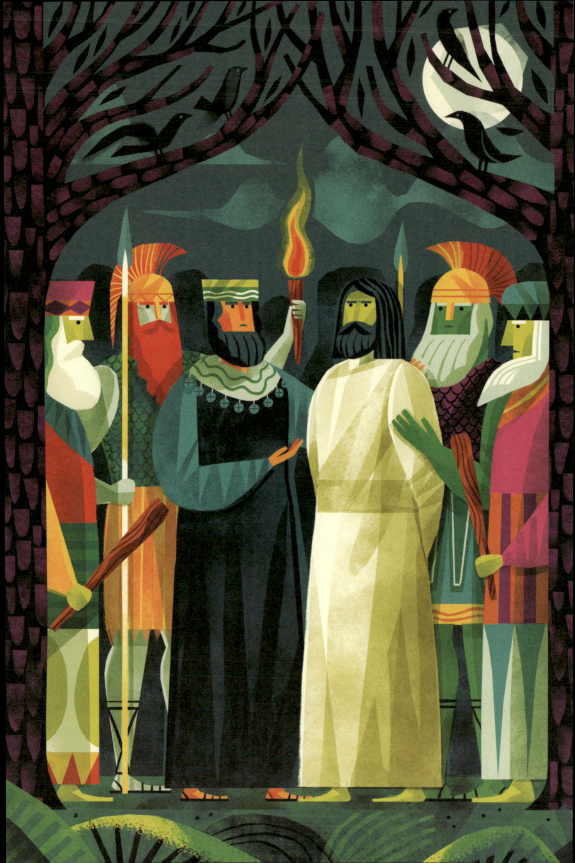

STORY 81

Everyone Leaves Jesus

MARK 14

THE BIG PICTURE: At least three times Jesus told the twelve that he would be betrayed, be arrested, suffer, and die. They heard him, but they didn't understand him. Even after the Passover meal, where Jesus used the bread and cup to point to his death, the twelve couldn't yet grasp why Jesus's blood would have to be poured out for the forgiveness of sins. They wouldn't really understand who Jesus was and what he was doing that Passover Week until after his resurrection and the gift of the Holy Spirit. On the night before Jesus died, all the apostles turned against Jesus when he most needed them. Judas betrayed him. Peter denied him. And the other ten left him journey to the cross alone.

READING 1 • MARK 14:22–31

Jesus's Shocking Statement in the Last Supper

After the Passover meal, what did Jesus say about his closest friends? How did Peter respond? Do you think you would have responded the same way?

....

....

....

READING 2 • MARK 14:32–42
Watch and Pray

Who did Jesus take with him to the garden of Gethsemane? What did Jesus pray for? Did the Father say yes to Jesus's prayer? Was Jesus okay with the answer no? What does this teach us about prayer? How did Peter, James, and John fail Jesus? How can we make sure we "watch and pray" so we don't fail Jesus in the same way or in other ways?

....

....

....

....

READING 3 • MARK 14:10–11, 43–46
Betrayed!

Who betrayed Jesus? What is so shocking about *who* betrayed Jesus? Why did Judas betray Jesus? Judas betrayed Jesus for a little amount of money. Would you be tempted to do what Judas did if someone paid you a lot—like a million dollars?

....

....

....

....

READING 4 • MARK 14:66–71
Denied!

How many times did Peter deny knowing Jesus? Why did he do that? Are there times when you are afraid of what people might think of you or do to you that you are tempted to deny knowing Jesus too?

READING 5 • MARK 14:72

Tears of Repentance

How did Peter feel after he denied Jesus? How do you feel when you disobey God? Whom did Jesus come to die for? What should we do when we sin?

GOSPEL CONNECTION: Peter cried after he denied Jesus because he was sad and sorry. He let fear get in the way of friendship (and faith!). Peter's tears that day would be wiped away in two days. He would repent of his sin, return to Jesus after the resurrection, and be a great leader in the early church. He would preach the gospel and perform amazing miracles. And he would learn that Jesus came to die for sinners like him. Life has a way of exposing just how sinful we are. Even Peter wasn't righteous or courageous enough to follow Jesus perfectly. He was a sinner. We are sinners. He needed a Savior. We need a Savior. Jesus was Peter's Savior, and he is our Savior!

PRAYER: Father, forgive us for the times we have denied Jesus or been too scared to follow him. Amen.

STORY 82

The Snake Crusher Is Crushed for Us

MARK 15

THE BIG PICTURE: All four Gospels slow down the story once Jesus gets to Jerusalem for the Passover. In Mark's Gospel, for example, he summarizes thirty-three years of Jesus's life in the first ten chapters. But the last week of Jesus's life gets six whole chapters. Talk about slowing down—six chapters to cover seven days! Why spend so much time telling us about the Last Supper, Jesus's betrayal, Jesus's arrest and trial, Jesus's sufferings before the cross, and finally Jesus's terrible death on the cross? The answer is because the cross matters. The cross stands at the center of the Christian story.

READING 1 • MARK 15:16–20

Jesus Is Mocked

Who mocked Jesus? How? Why? What they did was terrible. But if you took away their bad attitudes (we should never mock Jesus!), what about their words and actions is actually true?

....

....

....

Story 82 • The Snake Crusher Is Crushed for Us • 325

READING 2 • MARK 15:21–26

Jesus Is Crucified

What is the heaviest thing you have ever carried? How hard do you think it would be to carry a wooden cross that was taller and wider than a man? What is true about the charge that hung above Jesus's head on the cross?

....

....

....

....

READING 3 • MARK 15:27–31

Save Yourself

Jesus was mocked by the soldiers in the governor's headquarters, and now he is mocked (or "reviled") while hanging on the cross. Who mocks him? How? Would Jesus actually save anyone if he came down from the cross?

....

....

....

....

READING 4 • PSALM 22:1–8; MARK 15:33–36

Forsaken

When the people heard "Eloi, Eloi" (a word in Aramaic) they thought Jesus was calling out for Elijah to come rescue him. But (tough question!) what was really happening when he cried out the opening words of Psalm 22? When Jesus felt forsaken by his Father, he was taking on all the punishment for our sins. He was forsaken so we might be forgiven! Why then do we call the day Jesus died Good Friday?

READING 5 • MARK 15:37–39; HEBREWS 10:11–22

The Power of the Cross

When Jesus died, what happened to the curtain in the temple? If the curtain kept people from the Holy Place where God met with the high priest, what do you think it means that the curtain was torn when Jesus died? A centurion is a Roman soldier who leads a hundred soldiers. What is surprising and remarkable about what this important soldier said? Should we confess what he confessed about Jesus?

GOSPEL CONNECTION: The name Snake Crusher goes back to one of the earliest promises in the Bible, when God said to the serpent who deceived Eve in the garden of Eden, "Because you have done this, there will be a long and great struggle between you and Eve's offspring until the day when a child is born from her family, who will crush your head once and for all" (see Gen. 3:14–15). Jesus is the Snake Crusher. He is the son of Mary and the Son of God. But what is surprising in our story is that the Snake Crusher is crushed. Although he had never sinned, he was punished by God for all the sins of the world. Why? So we wouldn't have to be punished. Jesus was crushed so we don't have to be crushed. He took the punishment for us. What a Good Friday!

PRAYER: Our loving Lord Jesus, we thank you for your sacrifice on the cross. You were crushed so we might be saved. Amen.

STORY 83

Jesus Lives

LUKE 24

THE BIG PICTURE: On Friday Jesus died. So dark and sad. On Saturday his body lay in the tomb—totally dark, sad, and silent. On Sunday, however, as the sun rose in the sky, the Son of God rose from the grave. The first to witness the resurrection were a few women. They didn't expect Jesus to be alive. We know this because they brought spices to the tomb. Dead bodies don't smell so good, so they wanted to make Jesus's body smell better. But when they arrived, they found that the huge stone in front of the tomb was rolled away and Jesus's body was not there. Surprise of all surprises! Just then, another surprise. Two angels stood before them and announced, "Why do you seek the living among the dead? He is not here, but has risen." (Luke 24:5–6). Jesus is alive!

READING 1 • LUKE 23:50–24:12

The Empty Tomb

What did the women come to the tomb to do? Did they think Jesus would be alive or dead? What did the two men in dazzling apparel (angels) tell them? Did the apostles at first believe what the women told them?

READING 2 • LUKE 24:13–24

On the Road to Emmaus

Why couldn't the men talking with Jesus recognize him? Did they believe what the women said about Jesus?

READING 3 • LUKE 24:25–27

Foolish

What is something foolish you have done—or something someone in your family has done? Why did Jesus call the two disciples on the road to Emmaus, "O foolish ones" (Luke 24:25)? Are we foolish if we do not believe what the Bible says about Jesus's sufferings and resurrection?

READING 4 • LUKE 24:28–34

Opened Eyes

Did they recognize Jesus by their own power or God's power? Why do you think God linked Jesus's breaking bread and their understanding of who broke the bread? Does your heart ever burn when God's word is explained to you?

....

....

....

READING 5 • LUKE 24:36–48

See My Hands

Why did Jesus ask for food? The Law of Moses, the Prophets, and the Psalms are a Jewish way of talking about the three parts of the Old Testament. Does the Old Testament talk about Jesus? What specifically? When we share the gospel what should we make sure we share?

....

....

....

....

GOSPEL CONNECTION: Remember when Jesus said to the two men on the road, "O foolish ones, and slow of heart to believe all that the prophets have spoken! Was it not necessary that the Christ should suffer these things and enter into his glory?" (24:25–26). Then, starting with Genesis and ending with the prophets, he taught them from the Old Testament about himself. "It was written," Jesus said "that I should rise from the dead and that the good news that sins are forgiven should be preached to all the nations" (see 24:27). Jesus rose from the dead, just like the Old Testament said. Those two followers then understood and believed. And that is the good news we should believe too!

PRAYER: We thank you, God, for Jesus's glorious resurrection! Open our eyes to understand how the Bible points to what he has done for us. Amen.

STORY 84

A Mission for the Ages

MATTHEW 28

THE BIG PICTURE: Three days after Jesus was crucified, he turned the world upside down (or right side up): he rose from the dead. He is alive! He appeared to the women at the tomb, the two men on the road outside Jerusalem, and all the apostles. In fact, Paul tells us "he appeared to more than five hundred brothers [Christians] at one time" (1 Cor. 15:6), and then later to Paul himself. Over five hundred people. Wow! That's a lot of eyewitnesses! One of the times Jesus appeared to his disciples, he said something very important to them. He wanted them to be more than eyewitnesses; he wanted them to tell the world what they had seen and heard.

READING 1 • MATTHEW 28:1–9
Go to Galilee

What did the angel say to the women about Jesus? Where did the angel tell the women to tell the apostles to meet Jesus? As they were running to tell them, who did they meet and what did they do? Why do you think they grabbed his feet?

....

....

....

READING 2 • MATTHEW 28:16–17

Reactions to the Resurrected Christ

Why do you think Jesus met the apostles (minus Judas) on a mountain in Galilee? How did they react when they saw him? How would you have reacted?

....

....

....

READING 3 • MATTHEW 28:18

Jesus's Power

How much authority does Jesus have? Over what? How does knowing that Jesus has "all authority in heaven and on earth" help you pray, share your faith, and live through hard times?

....

....

....

....

READING 4 • MATTHEW 28:19

Go!

Have you ever been to a baptism? If so, what did you see and think? Those who receive the gospel are baptized with water into "the name of the Father and of the Son and of the Holy Spirit"? How many persons is our God? How important is it that God is Trinity—three persons, one God? How many nations should hear the good news about Jesus?

....

....

READING 5 • MATTHEW 1:23; 28:20

Jesus's Presence

Who is with his church always? How does Immanuel's presence (God the Son is with us!), help the church fulfill its mission? We are to teach the nations to know and keep Jesus's commandments. Can you think of one of Jesus's commandments that you would share with someone if they wanted to follow Jesus?

GOSPEL CONNECTION: The final command Jesus gave was so important that we call it the Great Commission. The word "commission" just means "command." And what is the Great Commission? Jesus commanded this, "Go therefore and make disciples of all nations." He wanted to make it clear that he didn't just come to rescue his Jewish disciples. He came to rescue people from every country, language, and group of people. What a *great* command indeed! And the best part is this: if Jesus—who has all authority over everything—tells us to do something, we can be sure he will help us complete that task. In fact, he promises to be with us always! As we tell people about how they can be rescued by Jesus and how he has crushed the snake, we help accomplish his mission to rescue people from every nation.

PRAYER: We thank you Father, Son, and Holy Spirit that we can know you, worship you, and tell other people how to follow you. Amen.

STORY 85

The Spirit Comes

ACTS 2

THE BIG PICTURE: Fifty days after Easter was Pentecost, a special feast day. When the apostles gathered in Jerusalem to celebrate with thousands of other people from around the world, suddenly a "mighty rushing wind" (Acts 2:2) from heaven came upon them. Then what looked like flames shaped like tongues of fire sat over each apostle's head. These tongues of fire were symbols that "they were all filled with the Holy Spirit." And because of that, they were able "to speak in other tongues" (2:4), or languages, about the mighty works of God. That day all the different people from all the different places heard the good news in their own language. Amazing!

READING 1 • ACTS 2:1–4

Suddenly . . . the Spirit

Do you know any other language besides English? If so, did it take a long time to learn? On the day of Pentecost, why were the apostles able to speak in other languages without ever learning those languages?

....

....

....

READING 2 • ACTS 2:5–13

What Does This Mean?

What did the devout Jews from every nation hear? How did they respond? How would you respond if you were there and heard a man who doesn't know English speaking in English about the mighty works of God?

....

....

....

....

READING 3 • ACTS 2:14–21

Peter's Sermon

What did Peter say was happening? What will happen to everyone who calls on the Lord?

....

....

....

....

READING 4 • ACTS 2:22–24, 36

Hear These Words

What did Peter preach about Jesus? When people teach or preach about Jesus and they just share about his miracles, what is missing?

....

....

....

READING 5 • ACTS 2:37–41

What Shall We Do?

How did Peter answer the people's question? Should we respond to the gospel in the same way? In the Old Testament Pentecost was a feast that God's people offered thanksgiving for the first part of the wheat harvest. What kind of "harvest" happened at the Pentecost in Acts 2?

....

....

....

....

GOSPEL CONNECTION: The prophet Joel had a vision of what it would be like when God's kingdom came on earth. In that vision God would pour out his Spirit on all people: men and women, young and old. Now that the Snake Crusher had come, that vision was coming true. It all began at Pentecost. The Spirit came down and enabled his followers to preach in different languages so that God's kingdom could spread. It spread and spread from that small group of disciples to all nations. The book of Acts tells the story of how the gospel spread from Jerusalem to every part of the world. Jesus's rescue mission had begun, and it cannot be stopped.

PRAYER: We thank you, God, for pouring out your Spirit so we can hear your word, repent, and believe. Amen.

STORY 86

The Beautiful and the Beggar

ACTS 3

THE BIG PICTURE: Shortly before Jesus died, he told his disciples something mind-blowing: "Whoever believes in me will also do the works that I do; and greater works than these will he do, because I am going to the Father" (John 14:12). After Jesus's resurrection, he ascended to the Father; then he sent the Holy Spirit. Once the Spirit filled God's people with God's power, the gospel spread around the world. And, like Jesus, they did some amazing things that showed everyone that a new time in world history had arrived. Let's learn about an example of those greater works.

Watch Story 86 together

READING 1 • ACTS 2:42–47
A Beautiful Picture of the Early Church

What were the four things mentioned in verse 42 that the early church in Jerusalem devoted themselves to? Should churches today devote themselves to the same? According to this passage, how does the church grow?

....

....

....

....

READING 2 • ACTS 3:1–2

At the Beautiful Gate

Do you know someone who cannot walk? You might think, "Sure, my baby sister, or my great grandfather who needs a wheelchair." How was the lame man in this story different? Because he couldn't walk, he couldn't work. What did he do to get money so he might eat? How do you think you would feel if you needed to beg others for money?

READING 3 • ACTS 3:3–10

Rise Up and Walk

What did the man expect to receive from Peter and John? What did Peter give him instead? How did he and others respond?

READING 4 • ACTS 3:11–16

Who Gets the Glory

Did Peter and John receive the praise for this miracle? Whom did Peter turn the people's attention to? How is that a lesson for us when God does something amazing in our lives?

....

....

....

READING 5 • ACTS 3:17–26

The End of Peter's Sermon

What did Peter tell the people to do? Some of the men of Jesus's day were responsible for his death. But how are we also responsible? Do we, like them, need to repent?

....

....

....

....

GOSPEL CONNECTION: Peter's sermon didn't just explain why the man could now walk; it ended with the good news about the Snake Crusher. Peter told the people that they "delivered over the Holy and Righteous Author of Life and asked for Barabbas the murderer instead" (see Acts 3:13–15). Peter wanted them to understand that what they did was wrong. But thankfully, he didn't stop there. He told them the good news. "God raised Jesus from the dead and glorified him," Peter preached. "And we apostles are all witnesses! We saw these things with our own two (or, actually twenty-four!) eyes" (see 3:13, 15). He continued, telling them that Jesus suffered just like the prophets said he would and that now is the time to *repent*: *turn from* sin and *turn to* God. That same message—of bad then good news—is for us. He had to die because we are terrible sinners. But the good news is that if we repent and believe, God will forgive our sins, give us new life, and help us to walk with Jesus.

PRAYER: Lord God, forgive us of our sins. Help us to walk with Jesus all our days. Amen.

STORY 87

One Name under Heaven

ACTS 4

THE BIG PICTURE: Here's a simple equation (like 1 + 1 + 1 = 3) for how the church grows: power + preaching + persecution = growth. It makes sense that God's *power* is necessary, and *preaching* makes sense too (people need to hear the good news). But how does *persecution* (God's people suffering for the gospel) grow the church? It is a bit of a mystery, but the answer to the mystery is connected to Christ. He suffered, so we must suffer; he is raised to glory; we too one day will be raised to glory. So, all that to say, *keep an eye out* for another sermon, *see* how many people our powerful God saves, and *watch* what happens when the apostles run into some persecution.

READING 1 • ACTS 4:1–4
Church Growth

Why were the religious leaders upset with Peter and John? Do you know people today who get upset when you or others share about Jesus? What happened to Peter and John? While in prison, what must have brought joy to their hearts?

....

....

....

READING 2 • ACTS 4:5–12

A Good Question, a Better Answer

How did Peter answer the question, "By what power or by what name did you [heal the man who could not walk]" (Acts 4:7)? When Peter said that "there is salvation in no one else [but Jesus]" because there is "no other name under heaven . . . by which we must be saved" (4:12), what did he mean? How important is it to believe that Jesus is the only way to God?

READING 3 • ACTS 4:13–22

We Cannot but Speak

Were Peter and John bold about their faith because they were physically strong and well educated? Who gives us the power we need to be bold? Why did Peter and John refuse to listen to the authorities? When is it right to obey the authorities and when is it wrong?

READING 4 • ACTS 4:23–31

An Important Prayer

Do you find it hard or easy to share Jesus with others? What did the early church pray for? How can their prayer help us to know what to pray for?

....

....

....

....

READING 5 • ACTS 4:32–37

Another Beautiful Picture

When the early church was gathered together in Jerusalem, with many people far from home, what did they need to do? What does their sacrifice teach us today about how we should help people in need in our church?

....

....

....

....

GOSPEL CONNECTION: The night before the Snake Crusher went to the cross to crush sin and Satan, he said, "I am the way, and the truth, and the life. No one comes to the Father except through me" (John 14:6). What he meant by that is what Peter preached: that the only way to be saved is to trust in Jesus. So when people say there are many ways to God, we are to say, "No way! There is only one way!" And when people say, "I will go to heaven because I'm a good person," we should say, "Only Jesus is perfectly good. We must believe in him and his perfect goodness alone."

PRAYER: Jesus, you are the only Savior. We love you, and we need you. Amen.

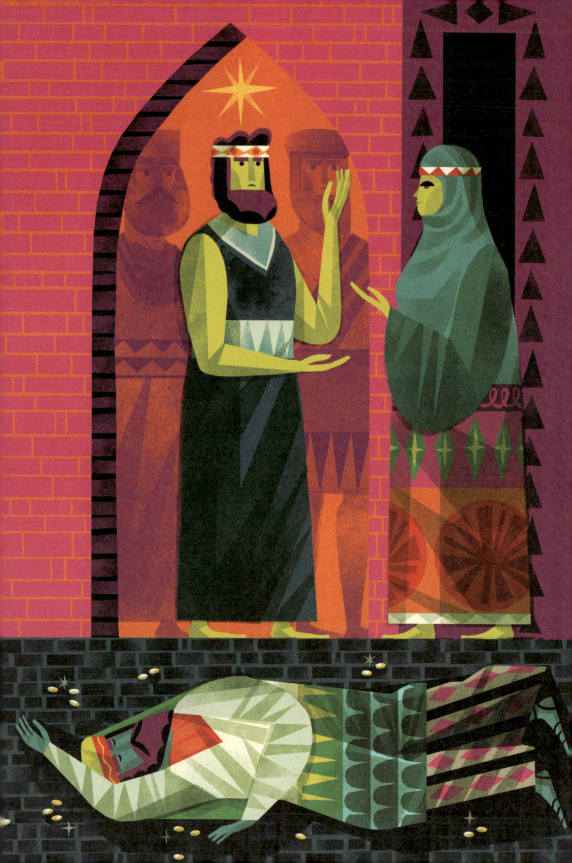

STORY 88

The Couple Who Lied and Died

ACTS 5

THE BIG PICTURE: So many wonderful things were happening! Thousands of people were coming to Christ as they heard the preaching of the apostles. Among those thousands there were many needs. So one way to provide for others was for people to share what they owned. Some opened their homes and provided shelter; others shared food and clothing; still others made bigger sacrifices. How wonderful! But that paved the way for the terrible thing. Ananias and Sapphira, a couple in the community, sold some land to give to the church. What a sacrifice! Ah, but what a scam. They decided to sell the land, keep some of the money from the sale, give some money to the church, and then lie about the fact that they kept some for themselves.

READING 1 • EXODUS 20:1–3

Review

The first command of the Ten Commandments is "You shall have no other gods before me" (Ex. 20:3). Do you remember the other nine? If so, recite them (or try to recite them). Do you remember the ninth commandment, about always telling the truth? Do you think all God's commands to his people are important?

READING 2 • ACTS 5:1–4

A Little Lie?

Were Ananias and Sapphira doing something good for other Christians? What was wrong with what they did?

READING 3 • ACTS 5:5–10

Lying to God!

What happened to Ananias? Is this what always happens when someone lies? Why do you think it happened at this time in history? Did Sapphira know what happened to her husband? What happened to her? What is your gut reaction to what happened?

READING 4 • ACTS 5:5, 11

Great Fear

After both deaths, we read about a "great fear" that came upon the church. Is it always bad to be afraid of God? How can a right fear of God's holiness and power help us in our Christian walk?

READING 5 • HEBREWS 6:18

Something God Cannot Do

What is impossible for God to do? How about you? Have you ever lied? (Now don't lie about your answer!) Would God be just if he judged you right now for lying, or any other sin? Who paid for all our sins, including all our lies?

GOSPEL CONNECTION: God is a truth teller. Satan is the opposite. As Jesus taught, Satan "does not stand in the truth, because there is no truth in him. . . . He is a liar and the father of lies" (John 8:44). And the Bible says that people who act like the father of lies by lying all the time will be thrown, with Satan, "in the lake that burns with fire and sulfur, which is the second death" (Rev. 21:8). Those who make a practice of lying will die and be sent to hell. We don't want that. So what do we do? Stop lying! Sure, but, no one (except Jesus) can live his or her whole life without lying. Jesus alone is "the truth" (John 14:6). So we escape hell not by never lying but by lying down at the feet of Christ—trusting that the Snake Crusher crushed all our sins.

PRAYER: Dear God, help me to tell the truth—always, no matter the cost, and no matter how small the lie may seem to me. Amen.

STORY 89

Stephen's Speech

ACTS 7

THE BIG PICTURE: The day before Jesus died, he told the apostles, "If the world hates you, know that it has hated me before it hated you" (John 15:18). Acts teaches us that his first followers were hated, just like Jesus had said. Some of them were also killed! One of the earliest Christians who was killed for testifying about Jesus was Stephen. He was a servant in the church, caring for the basic needs of others. He was also a "man full of faith and of the Holy Spirit" (Acts 6:5), someone who performed great wonders and preached bold sermons. But it was one of his bold sermons about Jesus that got him killed!

READING 1 • ACTS 6:8–15

Stephen Is Seized

What was Stephen doing? Why was Stephen seized (captured) and brought before the Jewish council?

....

....

....

....

READING 2 • ACTS 7:1–8
Are These Things So?

Stephen was accused of speaking about the temple ("the holy place") and "the law" of Moses—the first five books of the Bible. So when Stephen was asked to give a defense, who were the three men in Israel that he started with? In what book of the Bible do we find their stories?

....

....

....

....

READING 3 • ACTS 7:17–22, 30–34
Down to and out of Egypt

One person falsely testified that Stephen spoke against Moses. This is why Stephen started with the promises to Abraham, Isaac, and Jacob. He next talked about the story of Joseph and how Israel got down to Egypt. He talked about the book of Genesis! After that, whose story and what book of the Bible did he go to?

....

....

....

....

READING 4 • ACTS 7:44–50
Talk of the Temple

After Stephen shared about how God used Moses to deliver his people from slavery in Egypt, he talked about how Israel rejected Moses ("Who made you a ruler?") and God ("They made a [golden] calf"). Next, he talked about the tabernacle in the days of Moses and temple in the time of Solomon. God commanded Israel to build a place to worship him. But does God need a place to be worshiped? Who is the true, living, and everlasting temple who is always with us?

READING 5 • ACTS 7:51–60

The Stoning of Stephen

What happened to Stephen when he said that the religious leaders betrayed and murdered Jesus, the Righteous One? What is surprising about what Stephen saw and said before he died? Do you think you would have such courage to say and do what he said and did?

GOSPEL CONNECTION: In Stephen's sermon he talked about how Moses was rejected, just like all the prophets God sent were rejected. In Isaiah 53 the prophet Isaiah wrote about Jesus: "He was despised and rejected by men" (Isa. 53:3) Isaiah also went on to say that Jesus "carried our sorrows" (53:4) and that he was "crushed" (53:5) on the cross. But the good news was that when he was crushed on the cross, our sins were forgiven ("He bore the sin of many" people, 53:12). And because he suffered, we have been made well ("With his wounds we are healed," 53:5). *Jesus's rejection is our salvation*. What good news! Let us, like Stephen, boldly share that gospel with others, no matter if they hate us or hurt us.

PRAYER: Righteous Jesus, help me to never be silent about you and your love for sinners. Amen.

STORY 90

Philip and the Man from Africa

ACTS 8

THE BIG PICTURE: Jesus told his disciples to take the good news to Jerusalem, Judea, and Samaria. As the church fled from persecution in Jerusalem, they next went to Judea and Samaria. The first person to preach the gospel in Samaria was Philip. Like Stephen, Philip was a servant who cared for the needs of others. He was also someone who, through the Spirit's power, performed amazing miracles and preached great sermons. He preached "the gospel to many villages of the Samaritans" (Acts 8:25), and many people believed and were baptized. He also went on a special mission to take the word to one special man from Africa.

READING 1 • ACTS 8:26–31
The Start of an Incredible Journey

What do we learn about this man who was traveling down from Jerusalem? Who directed Philip to go to him? Have you ever been in a desert? If so, what was it like? If not, what do you imagine it might be like?

....

....

Story 90 • Philip and the Man from Africa • 357

READING 2 • ACTS 8:29–31

Need Help?

Even though the Ethiopian had his own copy of the book of Isaiah (which must have been expensive back then), did he need help understanding what the prophet taught? Do you ever find the Bible hard to understand? Who helps you understand it?

READING 3 • ISAIAH 53:1–8; ACTS 8:32–35

Like a Sheep Led to Slaughter

The Ethiopian was reading from Isaiah 53. What did he find confusing? How do you think Philip explained "the good news about Jesus" through the passage?

READING 4 • ACTS 8:36–40

Here Is Water!

How important was baptism to the message Philip preached? Do you think all Christians should be baptized? Have you been baptized? If not, do you want to be baptized?

READING 5 • 1 PETER 2:19–25

The Suffering Servant

Isaiah 53 is an important passage! It is so important that it is quoted seven times in the New Testament. The last time is in 1 Peter 2:19–25. How does the fact that Jesus suffered unjustly (in a way that was not fair) help us to endure through tough times, especially if we are treated unfairly for our faith?

GOSPEL CONNECTION: Last Gospel Connection we also talked about Isaiah 53 and how the Snake Crusher, before he crushed the snake, would suffer for our sin and carry all our sorrows as he was killed on the cross. Jesus's trial was not fair. He did not deserve to suffer the way he did. He was an innocent man sent to die. But, once again, this was God's wise plan. God took what was really bad and turned it into something really good. The "sheep" who was slaughtered brought all who believe in him life! No wonder the Ethiopian rejoiced to learn about Jesus!

PRAYER: Our good God, thank you for parents and pastors who can teach us the Bible and about the suffering servant, who came to suffer for our sins. Amen.

STORY 91

Saul Sees the Light

ACTS 9

THE BIG PICTURE: When Stephen was stoned, a man named Saul was there and he approved of the whole thing. How awful! What is just as awful is what he wanted to do next. Because he was "still breathing threats and murder against the disciples of the Lord" (Acts 9:1)—described here like a raging bull, with eyes aflame, smoke coming out of his nose, and ready to charge—he went to Damascus so he might capture Christians and bring them back to Jerusalem to be sentenced "to death" (26:9–11). What a merciless murderer on a merciless mission. Who will put a stop to him? And how? Jesus put a stop to Saul's merciless mission! How? By showing him mercy.

Watch Story 91 together

READING 1 • ACTS 8:1–3; 9:1–2

Breathing Murder

What was Saul doing? Why do you think he was doing that? Do really religious people do really bad things because they really don't understand what God is doing?

....

....

....

Story 91 • Saul Sees the Light • 361

READING 2 • ACTS 9:3–9

Blinded by the Light

Who was Saul throwing into prison? Who did Jesus say that Saul was persecuting? How does what Jesus says here—that if you persecuting the church you are persecuting him—teach us about his connection with his people?

....

....

....

....

READING 3 • ACTS 9:10–16

God's Chosen Instrument

Who is someone you know who you think would *never* become a Christian? If God can choose to save Saul, can he choose to save anyone? God not only saved Saul (later called Paul) but gave him a very important job. What did he call him to do?

....

....

....

....

READING 4 • ACTS 9:17–18a

New Sight

Why do you think Saul was blinded? How did God decide to give back Saul's sight? What was the lesson for him, Ananias, and us?

....

READING 5 • ACTS 9:18b–22

Amazing Grace

After Saul's eyes were opened, he was baptized and ate some food. What else did he do? Can God turn a persecutor against Christians into a Christian preacher? Is there anyone you know (even the worst person) who is too far from the reach of God's grace?

GOSPEL CONNECTION: In Paul's many letters he wrote about his life before and after his Damascus road experience. Before he encountered Jesus, he was "a blasphemer, persecutor, and insolent opponent" (1 Tim. 1:13), someone who "persecuted the church of God violently and tried to destroy it" (Gal. 1:13). Jesus saved Saul to show patience and mercy and to show that no one is too bad to be saved. Anyone who confesses that he is a sinner (however big or small the sins), asks for forgiveness, and believes that the Snake Crusher died for him can be saved. That's what's so great about the gospel. Paul put it this way: "The saying is trustworthy and deserving of full acceptance, that Christ Jesus came into the world to save sinners, of whom I am the foremost" (1 Tim. 1:15). God's grace knows no limits.

PRAYER: Thank you, our gracious God, for saving Saul and for saving us. Help us to see and believe. Amen.

STORY 92

Peter Eats and a Soldier Believes

ACTS 10

THE BIG PICTURE: The book of Acts uses two whole chapters to tell and retell the story of Cornelius's coming to Christ. In some ways, it is the same story as Saul's: God's grace reached down and saved someone. But in other ways, the two stories are worlds apart. Saul was a very serious Pharisee (a Jew) who did some seriously sinful things. And before Jesus saved him from his sins, he persecuted Christians and was on a terrible mission to destroy Christianity. Cornelius was a Roman soldier (a Gentile) who was a good man who was seeking after the God of Israel. God saved them both. His grace has no limits!

READING 1 • ACTS 10:9–16; 11:5–9
A God-Directed Plan

At the beginning of Acts 10 the Roman centurion Cornelius had a vision that directed him to find Peter. What happened to Peter the next day? Do you think God still directs people today through visions? What is something that you were served for a meal that you refused to eat? Why was Peter reluctant to eat certain kinds of reptiles and birds? What did God want Peter to see?

....

....

....

....

READING 2 • ACTS 10:17–23a
What the Spirit Said

What did the Holy Spirit say to Peter? Did he obey?

....

....

....

READING 3 • ACTS 10:23b–33; EPHESIANS 2:11–16
Broken Down the Wall

What were the two things that Peter told Cornelius, a Gentile, were "unlawful" for a Jew (like him) to do? In Jesus how did God break down the wall that separated Jews and Gentiles?

....

....

....

....

READING 4 • ACTS 10:34–43
Peter Preaches

According to Peter, could Gentiles be a part of God's kingdom? In Peter's short sermon (or Luke's summary of a long sermon) he talks a lot about Jesus. What did he want Cornelius (and us too!) to know about Jesus?

READING 5 • ACTS 10:44–48; 11:15–18; EPHESIANS 2:17–22

The Spirit Falls

What happened at the end of Peter's sermon on Jesus? What does the Holy Spirit's falling on Cornelius tell us about who the gospel is for? After Cornelius (and his family and friends) were baptized in the Spirit, what did they do next?

GOSPEL CONNECTION: We know that God is holy and people are sinful because of one of the first stories in the Bible—when Adam and Eve ate the forbidden fruit and God sent them out from the garden of Eden. We know that Jesus died for sinners because Matthew, Mark, Luke, and John tell us the story. And we know that sinners can find forgiveness and eternal life by believing in him through stories like Saul and Cornelius. More than that, we learn through their stories that God's grace knows no limits. Even the worst of sinners, like Saul, can be saved; and even Roman soldiers, like Cornelius, can be saved. The wideness of God's mercy includes all people from all nations—whoever trusts in Jesus!

PRAYER: God of Abraham, we thank you for bringing together Jews and Gentiles through the gospel. Amen.

STORY 93

Knock Knock, Who's There?

ACTS 12

THE BIG PICTURE: Have you ever been stuck somewhere, and you didn't know how to get out? Maybe you were scared. Maybe you needed your parents to help you get out. Well, Peter found himself stuck somewhere (a prison cell), and his parents weren't going to get him out of this one. He was there because Herod was laying his "violent hands on some who belonged to the church" (Acts 12:1). He killed James. He had his head cut off! He also "seized" (captured) Peter and "put him in prison," and had "four squads of soldiers to guard him" (12:4). He made sure there would be no escape. Ah, but he didn't count on who he was up against.

READING 1 • ACTS 12:1–5

Horrid Herod

What happened to James? Does God always rescue (in this life) everyone who serves him faithfully? What did the church do once they found out what happened to Peter?

....

....

....

READING 2 • ACTS 12:5–11

Answered Prayer

Do you have any prayers that have been answered lately? How did God answer his people's prayers for Peter? What do you find to be most interesting about Peter's prison escape?

....

....

....

....

READING 3 • ACTS 12:12–17

Out of Prison

What was the church gathered in Mary's house doing when Peter knocked on the door? What funny thing did Rhoda do? Once Peter was finally let in the house, what did he share?

....

....

....

....

READING 4 • ACTS 12:18–19

The Next Day

What did Herod do with the prison guards? Why did he do that? How would you like to work for Herod?

....

....

READING 5 • ACTS 12:20–25

Struck Down

Herod was so wicked and proud. In the end what happened to him? Did all his evil acts stop the message of the gospel? How do all the events in Acts 16 encourage us?

GOSPEL CONNECTION: There are lots of rescue stories in the Bible. As we just learned, God rescued Peter from Herod's violent hand. God also rescued Israel from the giant Goliath and Daniel from the lion's den. The biggest rescue in the Biggest Story, however, was when the Snake Crusher crushed Satan on the cross. God continues today to rescue his people, and one day soon, Jesus will come again and "rescue [us] from every evil deed and bring [us] safely into his heavenly kingdom" (2 Tim. 4:18). As we wait for Jesus to return, let's turn away from any idols or false gods (if we are worshiping people or things we shouldn't be) and turn to "the living and true God" (1 Thess. 1:9–10), the only God worthy of our worship.

PRAYER: Our living and true God, thank you for rescuing us. Thank you for answering prayers too. Amen.

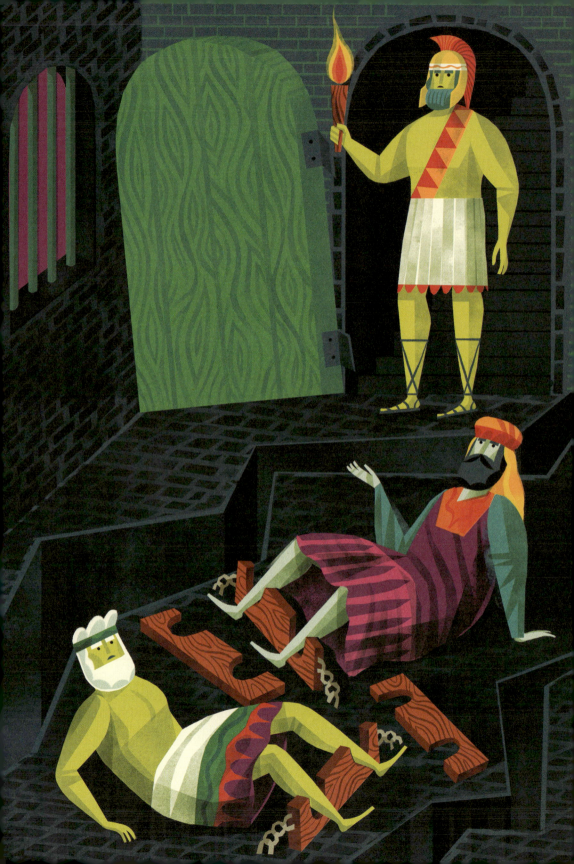

STORY 94

Paul, Purple Goods, and a Prison Quake

ACTS 16

THE BIG PICTURE: Rescue stories are awesome! The Bible is filled with awesome rescue stories. In the last lesson we heard how God rescued Peter from Herod, just like he saved Israel from the Egyptians. And, of course, we reminded ourselves of the biggest rescue in the Biggest Story—when the Snake Crusher crushed Satan on the cross. When God rescued Peter from prison, the guards who were supposed to be guarding him ended up in big trouble. When Herod discovered Peter was missing, he had all the guards killed! What is recorded in Acts 16 is about another God-powered prison break. But this time, something wonderful will happen to the jailer.

READING 1 • ACTS 16:1–10

Friendship and Calling

Why is it important to have good friends? Do you have a good friend? Who was the good friend that God gave to help Paul? Who was directing their mission?

....

....

READING 2 • ACTS 16:11–15

Lydia Listens

What did Paul do when he went to Philippi? Are you a good listener? Did Lydia become a Christian just because she was a good listener? What happened after she heard the gospel?

READING 3 • ACTS 16:16–24

More Persecution

What happened to Paul and his friend Silas? Why were they thrown into prison?

READING 4 • ACTS 16:25–31

What Must I Do to Be Saved?

If you were in prison with a good Christian friend, what would you do? What did Paul and Silas do? After the earthquake caused the doors to open and the prisoners' chains break, what did the jailer try to do and how did Paul stop him? What was Paul's answer the jailor's question?

....

....

....

....

READING 5 • ACTS 16:32–34

Rejoicing!

Who was baptized? Why? Why was everyone rejoicing that day?

....

....

....

....

GOSPEL CONNECTION: In God's kingdom to come everything will be perfect and no one will need to be rescued. But right now, there is a lot we need to be rescued from. The slave girl needed to be rescued from a demon, Paul needed to be rescued from prison, and the jailer needed to be rescued from sin and death. Only God can bring true rescue to us through Jesus. We might face evil forces, unfair punishment, or the pain that sin and death bring while we live now. But one day, if we believe in the Lord Jesus, we will be saved from all these things and live forever in God's perfect kingdom.

PRAYER: We thank you, God Most High, that we know the way to be saved. Give us faith to believe in the Lord Jesus, our Rescuer. Amen.

STORY 95

The God Who Can Be Known

ACTS 17

THE BIG PICTURE: Remember how Jesus saved Saul? That day on the road to Damascus, Paul's life was forever changed. And from that day forward he preached the gospel of Jesus Christ every day to everyone who would listen. He preached in cities and towns. He preached in synagogues, places where Jews gathered. He preached in the marketplace, places lots of people came to buy and sell. Over and over, place by place, person to person, he preached the gospel. In Acts 17 Paul preached a famous sermon to group of philosophers in the city of Athens. Let's hear what he says and see how they respond.

READING 1 • ACTS 17:10–15
On the Run

Why were some of the Jews from Thessalonica so upset with Paul and his friends? How can the way the Jews in Berea responded to the message be a model for us to follow?

....

....

....

READING 2 • ACTS 17:16–21

In Athens

What bothered Paul when he came to Athens? Do you ever get upset when you hear or see things that are against God's will? "The city was full of idols" (Acts 17:16), because the people of Athens believed that there were gods and goddesses to be prayed to for all sorts of things. People in our culture might not pray to idols and false gods, but who or what do they worship instead of the true and living God?

READING 3 • ACTS 17:22–28

Making the Unknown God Known

Why did the Athenians have an altar to an unknown god? What are some things that Paul shared about God? If you had to talk to someone who knew nothing about Christianity, where would you start the conversation?

READING 4 • ACTS 17:29–31

Repent!

What does it mean to repent? What was Paul calling them to repent of? Who was he calling them to believe in?

READING 5 • ACTS 17:32–34

Reactions

Did everyone who heard Paul's preaching believe the good news about Jesus? Will everyone whom we tell about Jesus believe the good news? Should we still tell people about Jesus?

GOSPEL CONNECTION: The Snake Crusher's death and resurrection stand at the center of the Biggest Story. We know that because all four Gospels end by talking about Jesus's death and resurrection. We also know that because every time Paul preached, he focused on Jesus's death and resurrection too. These truths stand at the center, because they are the heart of the gospel—good news for all people. And any time that gospel is preached and believed, lives are changed. Paul saw that happen time and time again. And if we believe the gospel, Jesus changes our lives too.

PRAYER: Lord of heaven and earth, we thank you for Paul's example. We believe in the resurrection. Help us to make good arguments for the good news we believe about Jesus. Amen.

STORY 96

Ships and Snakes and Sermons, Oh My!

ACTS 27–28

THE BIG PICTURE: At the beginning of Acts Jesus's disciples asked him about the kingdom, "Lord, will you now restore the kingdom of Israel?" (see Acts 1:6). Jesus gave an interesting answer. He talked about the Holy Spirit coming upon his disciples and how they would then take the message of the kingdom of God to *Israel* and to *the world*. Acts tells us how the gospel went to Jerusalem (remember how the Spirit came, Peter preached, and many believed?). Acts tells us how the gospel went to Samaria and then to the Gentiles (remember Cornelius?). By the end of Acts the gospel has reached the capital of the Roman Empire!

READING 1 • ACTS 27:1–2, 13–20

Sailing to Rome

Is it true that when Paul sailed to Rome, the weather was perfect and everyone was so happy? What was the weather like? How did everyone on board feel? Have you ever been on a boat in a storm or on a plane when there was turbulence that made the plane shake? How did you feel?

....

....

....

....

READING 2 • ACTS 27:21–25, 39–44

Paul's Plan

What did Paul promise if they listened to him? Did his plan work?

....

....

....

....

READING 3 • ACTS 28:1–10

Safe and Sound?

What happened to Paul on the island of Malta? Why did they want to worship him like he was a god? How did Paul help them?

....

....

....

....

READING 4 • ACTS 28:23–28

Arriving at Rome

Paul finally made to the capital city of the Roman Empire, Rome, and he lived by himself (well, also with a prison guard). One day, he was able to explain from the Bible about Jesus to some Jews. Did they believe him?

....

READING 5 • ACTS 28:30–31

Witnessing to the End

Since the day that Paul met Jesus on the road to Damascus, he preached the gospel to Jews and Gentiles the rest of his life. How does the book of Acts end? What lessons can we learn from Paul—both here at the end of Acts and soon the end of his life?

GOSPEL CONNECTION: Paul's journey on the ship is a great picture of what it can be like to follow Jesus. Sometimes we face great storms and we're scared of what is ahead. Even after Jesus brings us through the storm, we often face new challenges, like Paul being bit by the snake! When we follow Jesus, we will still face hard things. But because of Jesus we have hope of something better to come. Just like Paul, we too will make it to our promised destination—not Rome, but Home. The home Jesus has gone to prepare for us in heaven.

PRAYER: We praise you, O God, for the spread of the gospel across the whole world. Amen.

STORY 97

No Nothing

ROMANS 8

THE BIG PICTURE: Besides the Gospels and Acts, most of the New Testament is letters—short letters; long letters; letters from Peter, John, James, and Paul. Mostly Paul. Many of Paul's letters were written while Paul was in prison for sharing the gospel. And these letters are every bit as much about Jesus as the sermons and miracles in the Gospels and Acts. Perhaps the most famous letter that Paul wrote is his letter to the Romans. And perhaps the most famous chapter in his letter was chapter 8. It is so famous because it is so good. Well, it is so famous because God is so good!

READING 1 • ROMANS 8:1, 15–17

Children of God

Is there anything or anyone that can condemn us if we trust in Jesus? One day God's children will live with God. Does that wonderful promise mean that we don't need to suffer now? How are some ways you are suffering now?

....

....

....

....

READING 2 • ROMANS 8:18–25

Future Glory

Have you ever groaned? About what? What are some ways that the creation groans? As we groan now, what hope should we have?

....

....

....

....

....

READING 3 • ROMANS 8:26–30

All Things

How does the Spirit help? Do you believe that sad days and even tragedies that happen in your life are planned for your good?

....

....

....

....

....

READING 4 • ROMANS 8:31–34

God's Forever Love

How do we know for sure God loves us? Jesus not only died for us, but he intercedes for us. What does that mean? How does that help us in our daily life?

....

READING 5 • ROMANS 8:35–39

More Than Conquerors

If you had to pick one of the things mentioned that scares you most, what is it? Is there anything that can separate us from God's love?

GOSPEL CONNECTION: As long as we keep following Jesus, there is nothing that can separate us from God. Not death, not bad dreams, not bad people, not cancer, not car accidents, not things in the sky or things in the sea. Nothing. We know through Jesus that the snake has been crushed, that our sins have been paid for, and that death has been defeated. We have nothing to fear! We are safe. Safe in Jesus. If that isn't good news, then nothing is!

PRAYER: We praise you, our all-loving Lord, for your always-and-forever love for us in Jesus. Amen.

STORY 98

Love Is

1 CORINTHIANS 13

THE BIG PICTURE: The Bible says a lot about lots of important things—like peace, hope, faith, sin, and judgment. It also says a lot about love. Jesus said the most important commandment is to "love God with all your heart and with all your soul and with all your mind" and following from that to "love your neighbor as yourself" (Matt. 22:36–40; see Lev. 19:18; Deut. 6:5). Indeed, the Bible helps us see that love is the essential ingredient in the relationship between parents and children, between husbands and wives, between Christians, and even for Christians toward their enemies (even if enemies don't love us back!). It tells us that God loves us in Christ, just like we learned in Romans 8. A whole chapter of the Bible is devoted to love—1 Corinthians 13!

READING 1 • 1 CORINTHIANS 13:1–3

If We Have Not Love

What's the problem with the person who is really popular, really sure of God's promises, or really smart but who has no love for his neighbor? How does love change the way you think about others? How does it change the way you act toward others?

READING 2 • 1 CORINTHIANS 13:4–6

Love Is . . .

If someone says "Love is . . . ," how would you fill in the blank? In the next few verses God gives us his inspired definition. How is it unloving to do things like not waiting patiently, rudely interrupting someone, bragging about how great you are, or laughing when something bad happens to someone else?

READING 3 • 1 CORINTHIANS 13:7

All Things

What four things does love do? Take some time today (or right now!) to try to memorize 1 Corinthians 13:4–7.

READING 4 • 1 CORINTHIANS 13:8–12

In a Mirror

When Paul talks about being fully known and love never ending, he is talking about heaven, where we will be with God, who "is love" (1 John 4:8). He will love us and we will love him and others all the time for the rest of time. Sounds lovely! Take some time to think about that place. How will it be so different than our world now?

....

....

....

....

READING 5 • 1 CORINTHIANS 13:13

The Greatest

What are the three main Christian virtues? Why is love greater than faith and hope?

....

....

....

....

GOSPEL CONNECTION: On this fallen world, none of us loves perfectly. Most of us mess up a lot. So how can we love like Paul calls us to love? First John answers this for us: "We love because [God] first loved us" (1 John 4:19). We are only able to love when we have known God's love. The more we know God's love, the better we'll be able to love. John 3:16 says, "For God so loved the world, that he gave his only Son, that whoever believes in him should not perish but have eternal life." That means the way to know God's love is to know the gospel. Jesus died for us. The more we grasp how sinful we are, the more we grasp what Jesus did when he died for our sins, and the more we will love like Jesus did.

PRAYER: Dear God, you are love! Thank you that in Jesus we know love not just as something we do but as a person we can meet. Amen.

STORY 99

More Than a Slave

PHILEMON

THE BIG PICTURE: Paul wrote his letter to Philemon while he was in prison. Did Paul do something bad to wind up in prison? No! He was "a prisoner *for* Christ Jesus" (Philem. 1); that is, he was in a Roman prison because he was preaching the good news about Jesus. That was not right for the Romans to do. It was also not right to have slaves, and lots of Romans had slaves. The book of Philemon is written to a slave owner (Philemon) who became a Christian. So too did Philemon's runaway slave, Onesimus. Paul asked Philemon to free Onesimus because they were now *brothers* in Christ—together freed by Christ, equal in God's eyes, and fellow members of the church.

READING 1 • PHILEMON 1–3

Grace and Peace

What does Paul call himself? Why? This letter is written to Philemon, but who else is mentioned? Have you ever visited a house church, a church that meets in someone's house?

....

....

....

READING 2 • PHILEMON 4–7
Prayers of Thanksgiving

Why is Paul thankful? Do you ever thank God for others when you pray? Do you think that is a good idea to do?

READING 3 • PHILEMON 8–16
Paul's Plea (or Big Ask)

How do you think Onesimus, the runaway slave, became a Christian? Why is Paul sending Onesimus back to Philemon? How did Paul want Philemon to treat Onesimus—as a slave or a brother? How can Philemon and Onesimus be "brothers"?

READING 4 • PHILEMON 17–25
Refresh My Heart in Christ

If Onesimus owns Philemon anything (like money for not working as his slave), what does Paul say he will do? If you had the money, would you be generous in that way? Does Paul think Philemon should do what he asks him to do?

READING 5 • ROMANS 6:5–11

Set Free

What does Jesus's death set us free from?

GOSPEL CONNECTION: The Bible tells us that we have freedom in Christ. Does that mean that we don't have to listen to our parents? No. Does it mean we don't have to work for a boss? No. Does it mean Christians who are in prison, like Paul was, will be released? No. What it does mean is that, through Jesus's death, we have been "set free from sin" (Rom. 6:7) and the power of death. We are free to live now and forever for God. More than that (although that is quite a lot!) we are to "use [our] freedom" to "serve one another" (Gal. 5:13). Peter puts it this way: "Live as people who are free. Love your brothers and sisters in Christ" (see 1 Pet. 2:16–17).

PRAYER: Dear God, thank you for our freedom in Christ. We are free to love you and others. How blessed we are! Amen.

STORY 100

Taming the Tongue

JAMES 3

THE BIG PICTURE: There are thousands of words of wisdom between Genesis and Revelation! In the New Testament the book of James is known as a book of wisdom. It is filled with wise proverbs, like "Be doers of the word, and not hearers only" and "Draw near to God, and he will draw near to you" (James 1:22; 4:8). And James teaches us that wisdom from God is "first pure, then peaceable, gentle, open to reason, full of mercy and good fruits" (3:17). God's wisdom leads to peace with people! But we're not naturally people of peace. And James tells us the best clue of this is our terrible tongues.

Watch Story 100 together

READING 1 • JAMES 1:1–8
If You Lack Wisdom

James was Jesus's half-brother. They had the same mother—Mary. Yet, what does James call himself? What's surprising about that? How can we have joy when we are experiencing trials? What should we do when we need wisdom?

READING 2 • PROVERBS 10:31; 12:18; 15:2, 4; 21:23

The Wisdom and Folly of the Tongue

The book of Proverbs, like the book of James, teaches us about the power of our words. What are some ways to use our tongues foolishly? Wisely?

....

....

....

....

READING 3 • JAMES 3:1–5

The Small but Great

Why do you think Bible teachers will be "judged with greater strictness"? What is the power of the tongue compared to? Do you think our words are really that powerful? We all "stumble" or sin with our tongues. What is one way you most often stumble?

....

....

....

....

READING 4 • JAMES 3:5–12

Set Ablaze

If you lit a small match and tossed it into a big pile of dead, dry leaves in a forest where it hadn't rained in months, would the pile and then the trees likely catch fire? If no one put out the fire, would it burn a lot of trees? Why does James say that the "tongue is a fire"?

....

READING 5 • JAMES 3:13–18

Wisdom from Above

What kind of wisdom do we need to help us, not just to tame our tongues but to live peaceful lives with others? If we want to be wise, how will we use our tongues?

GOSPEL CONNECTION: James 2:10 essentially says: "If we keep all the commandments but disobey just one, we are guilty in God's eyes of breaking all of God's commandments." That means if, one day, we pray to God, go to church, obey our parents, share our toys, and don't scream and beg for candy at the checkout counter, but we yell "You're so dumb!" at our friend after she loses the board game, we are totally guilty. That means we're all guilty. And this is why we need the Snake Crusher. Only Jesus never sinned with his tongue. He always used his words to encourage people and praise his Father. And because he tamed his tongue, he was able to offer his body as the perfect sacrifice for our sins—even all our mean and unkind words. And if we believe in him and what he has done for us, then all our sins are forgiven. What good news!

PRAYER: Lord Jesus, help us to build people up with our words. Forgive us for the bad words we sometimes say and the bad things we sometimes say to others. Amen.

STORY 101

Jesus Writes a Letter

REVELATION 1–3

THE BIG PICTURE: Sometimes Revelation is called the Apocalypse. *Apocalypse* is the first word of the book, a Greek word that means "revelation." Revelation is a book that *reveals* many truths about Jesus, the church, and the world. It also reveals—through awesome (and crazy!) signs and symbols—truths about the past, present, and future. For example, it reveals that Jesus, the Lamb of God, conquered death through his death (the past), the church is now suffering for believing in Jesus (the present), and Jesus will return soon to judge evildoers and save all who trust in him (the future).

READING 1 • REVELATION 1:1–3
The Revelation

Have you ever had to cover your eyes because someone wanted to surprise you with something? When you opened your eyes, what was revealed? What is being revealed to John by Jesus?

....

....

....

....

READING 2 • REVELATION 1:4–8
To the Churches

Whom is John writing to? Whom is he writing about? What is said about who Jesus is and what he has done?

....

....

....

....

READING 3 • REVELATION 1:9–20
Falling at His Feet

Do you think of Jesus in the way that he is described here? How does how Jesus is pictured and talked about help expand your vision of him?

....

....

....

....

READING 4 • REVELATION 2:1–7
To the Church in Ephesus

The "seven churches that are in Asia" are the churches in the cities of Ephesus, Smyrna, Pergamum, Thyatira, Sardis, Philadelphia, and Laodicea (modern day Turkey). Perhaps a lot of what Jesus says in his first letter (to the church in Ephesus) is confusing. However, something you might understand is the promise he gives at the very end. What does Jesus promise for those who repent and press on in their faith? Do promises of great rewards—from Jesus, your parents, others—sometimes help you keep doing what is right and stop doing what is wrong?

READING 5 • REVELATION 3:14–22

A Knock at the Door

Usually, Jesus tells the church what they are doing right and then tells them what they need to stop doing and start doing. He does so because he loves them and wants them to change ("Those whom I love, I reprove and discipline," Rev. 3:19). Do adults in your life love you in the same way? What is the picture Jesus gives for what it would mean for the church in Laodicea to receive Jesus's loving discipline?

GOSPEL CONNECTION: Jesus's letters to the seven churches are like receiving a report card. If you receive a good report card, you feel good; if you receive a bad report card, you feel bad. Feeling bad isn't always bad. A kind teacher tells you where you fall short because she wants to help you grow, not because she wants you simply to feel bad. Jesus is better than the kindest teacher. He loves his church so much that he died for each and every Christian. He loves the church so much that he continues to tell us the truth about ourselves—so that he can help us grow. The way we become a Christian—turning *from* sin and *to* God—is what we need to do over and over throughout our Christian lives. Repent. Follow Jesus. Keep repenting and keep following Jesus.

PRAYER: Dear Lord, help us to be honest about ourselves, to keep going when we are right, and to turn the other way when we are wrong. Amen.

STORY 102

The Center of the Universe

REVELATION 4–5

THE BIG PICTURE: If you had to draw a picture that represented the fourth day of creation, when God created the lights in the sky (the sun, moon, and stars), what picture would you draw? Maybe a sunrise, or a half-moon with a few stars flickering around it. You can draw the sun, moon, and stars because you have seen those lights in the sky. You know what they look like, at least from a great distance. How about God? Can you draw a picture of God? We're not talking about drawing Jesus, who we all know is a human. How would you draw the eternal, invisible God, who is Spirit but not flesh? The book of Revelation gives us a picture of *that* God. Want to *see* it?

READING 1 • REVELATION 4:1–6a

A Door to Heaven

What does John see when he enters the door to heaven? How does this vision of God help us understand him better?

....

....

....

....

Story 102 • The Center of the Universe • 405

READING 2 • REVELATION 4:6b–11

Around the Throne

Who are the strange creatures around the throne? What do they say and do? Do you think they are ever bored? Why do you think you sometimes say, "I'm so bored"?

....

....

....

....

READING 3 • REVELATION 5:1–5

Who Is Worthy?

How many seals does the scroll have? Who cannot open the scroll? Who can? How is Jesus described?

....

....

....

....

READING 4 • REVELATION 5:6–10

Between the Throne

At the start of Revelation 5 Jesus is described as a powerful lion king. How is he described here? Why is Jesus worthy to open the scroll—what has he done? Who will be part of his perfect kingdom on earth?

....

....

READING 5 • REVELATION 5:11–14

Every Creature in Heaven and on Earth

What do those "around the throne" (in heaven) shout? After that, what then does "every creature in heaven and on earth and under the earth and in the sea" shout? What does the image of their worship teach us about God the Father and God the Son?

GOSPEL CONNECTION: We praise Jesus for the good news that he alone is holy enough to open the sealed scroll—and that he alone made the blood sacrifice on the cross that set sinners free from our slavery to sin. More than that, Jesus's death turned unholy people into holy priests. We don't make sacrifices in the temple, like priests in the Old Testament did. We sacrifice ourselves by giving our whole lives to God. And we don't do this alone. No, Jesus has gathered in his kingdom people from every nation around the world and throughout time. That's a big kingdom! That's a good kingdom. That's the perfect kingdom that every follower of Jesus will live in someday. That should make us want to shout and sing to our amazing God.

PRAYER: We worship you, God— Father, Son, and Holy Spirit—for you are holy. Help us to offer our lives as a sacrifice for you. Amen.

STORY 103

The Snake Crusher Wins

REVELATION 20

THE BIG PICTURE: On the island of Patmos, nearly two thousand years ago, the apostle John had a vision of Jesus. It was a strange vision of the *real* Jesus, who now rules as the King of kings, who rescues his church from evil, and who will come soon to judge the world. John saw what we today and always should see: Jesus the Lion (King), Jesus the Lamb (Savior), and Jesus the Snake Crusher (Judge). Yes, Jesus, who defeated death and conquered the grave, will soon judge and crush Satan. Yes, that slithering serpent of old—who accuses and tempts God's people and tells lies to the world—will be "thrown into the lake of fire" (Rev. 20:10). His day of doom is soon!

READING 1 • 1 JOHN 3:4–10

One Big Reason

According to this part of John's letter, why did Jesus come? Given that the Son of God appeared to "destroy the works of the devil," do God's children act like Satan (make a practice of sinning) or like Jesus (practice righteous or godly living)?

....

....

READING 2 • REVELATION 20:1–3
The Serpent Is Seized

Have you ever touched a snake? Who is the dragon, the ancient serpent? What happened to him? What is this a picture of?

READING 3 • REVELATION 20:4–6
Reign with Christ

How many years was Satan bound? How many years do faithful Christians rule with Christ? Do you think the number 1,000 is symbolic?

READING 4 • GENESIS 3:15; REVELATION 20:7–10
The Biggest Loser

How is the final defeat of Satan and all who follow him described? Does this picture of the Snake Crusher destroying evil give you hope?

READING 5 • REVELATION 20:11–15

Before the Great White Throne

Who is the Judge on the throne? Who will stand before his great white throne? What book do our names need to be written in to live forever and escape the lake of fire? Knowing what you know from the book of Revelation and the rest of the New Testament, how do we get our names written in that book?

GOSPEL CONNECTION: What is described in Revelation 20 can be scary. Are you afraid of the lake of fire? God's judgment throne? Can you imagine each and every sinful thought, word, and deed being read aloud when people stand before God on judgment day? Scary stuff! We should all fear God. He is an awesome, powerful, and holy God. But if we believe in Jesus, we don't need to be afraid. Or to use the images above, if our names are written in the book of life, our future will not be filled with fear but a feast! Revelation 21 describes heaven as being like a wonderful banquet. An all-you-can-and-want-to-eat-forever wedding feast. And who's getting married? Everyone who has followed Jesus. The church is "the Bride, the wife of the Lamb" (21:9).

PRAYER: Jesus, you win! How wonderful! And you will love us forever, like a husband loves his bride. How totally amazing. Thank you. Amen.

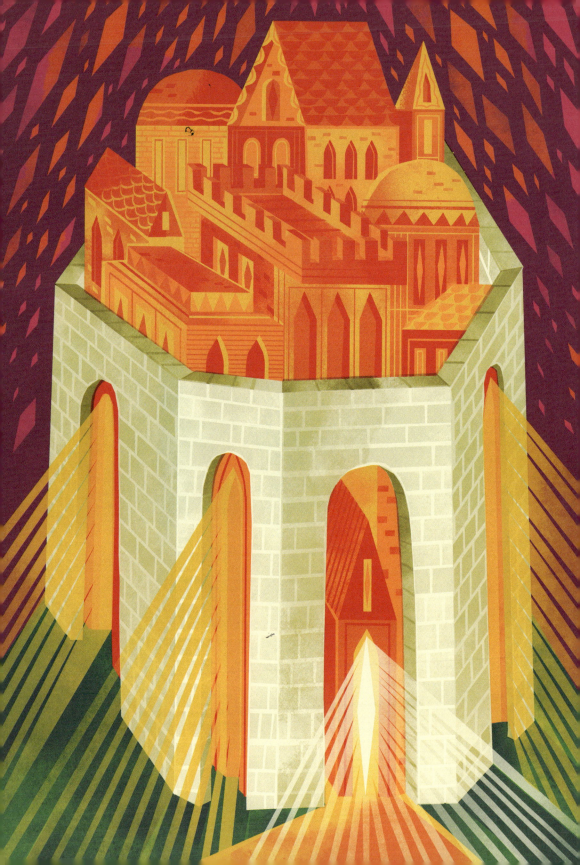

STORY 104

All Things New

REVELATION 21–22

THE BIG PICTURE: On the first six days, God created the sun, moon, stars, the sky, land, plants, trees, the sea, and every creature in heaven, on earth, and under the earth. This included humans—God's good people living in God's good land and ruling over God's good creation. On the last day of the first heavens and earth, God will judge every human. Revelation *shows* us that those who reject Jesus will go to everlasting destruction and those who trust him as Savior and bow before him as King will go to everlasting life. Revelation also *shows* us the place where God's people ("the Bride . . . of the Lamb," Rev. 21:9) will live. But the last day of the first heavens and earth will be the first day of the new heavens and earth. A new beginning!

READING 1 • REVELATION 21:1–4

The Dwelling Place

After evil is judged, where will God's people live? Whom will they live with? Without Satan, sin, suffering, and death, will it be a place of perfect joy?

....

....

READING 2 • REVELATION 21:9–14, 22–27
The New City on a Hill

What is unusual about the new Jerusalem? Does every human being ever made get to live in this city forever? Does God's judgment scare you, comfort you, or both?

READING 3 • GENESIS 2:8–17; REVELATION 22:1–5
A Better Eden

How does this picture of the dwelling place with God remind you of the garden of Eden? How is this place better then Eden?

READING 4 • REVELATION 22:6–7
Trustworthy and True

What is trustworthy and true? Who do you think says, "And behold, I am coming soon"?

READING 5 • REVELATION 22:12–20

Coming Soon

What does Jesus mean when he promises that he is coming soon? Do you think much about Jesus coming to earth again? How do we prepare for his second coming?

GOSPEL CONNECTION: We can summarize the Son of God's mission on earth with six key events: (1) He left heaven for earth. (2) He was born of Mary. (3) He lived a life without sin, healed the sick, cast out demons, taught truths, and welcomed people to follow him. (4) He suffered and died on behalf of sinners. (5) He rose from the grave. (6) Someday soon he will come again to gather his people, judge evil, and renew creation. Isn't Jesus amazing? Yes! Shouldn't we praise him? Yes! And shouldn't we long for the day when he returns? Yes, or Amen. "Amen, Come Lord Jesus!" (Rev. 22:20).

PRAYER: Please return to earth soon, our Lord Jesus. We long to see you and be with you forever! Amen.

CONTRIBUTORS

General Editor
Kevin DeYoung
PhD, University of Leicester

Artist & Illustrator
Don Clark

Editorial Team
Elliott Pinegar, Gerard Cruz, Davis Wetherell

Animation Director
Phil Borst

Animation Team
Anna Grace Botka, Kevin Botka, Nick Chiodras, Jon Marshall, Kyle Martinez

Family Devotional Author
Douglas Sean O'Donnell
PhD, University of Aberdeen

Creative Directors
Josh Dennis, Dan Farrell

Production Designer
Jared Hughes

Digital Team
Matt Ratleph, Micah Lanier, Adam Zapletal, Ben Cail

Music Composer
Grant Fonda

Animation Narrator
Michael Reeves

Notes: